# Preface—
## The Mystery
## Beneath the Surface

There's something about an old tale that stirs the soul. We lean in closer when the fire crackles, when shadows flicker on the wall, and someone begins, "You may not believe this, but..." It's as if our hearts know there's more to this world than what we can touch. The unexplainable. The supernatural. The hidden world beneath the surface of everyday life. These are not just curiosities; they are signposts pointing to something deeper.

We've always been drawn to mysteries. To creatures of the deep, unsolved disappearances, and legends whispered through generations. The stories of heroes rising against impossible odds, of ancient forces both light and dark. We hunger for these truths-not merely because they entertain, but because something inside us knows they are reflections of a greater reality.

This book is not the beginning of the tale.

If you've stumbled upon Frogman Puck: Resurgent without reading The Rising Tides, you've already missed the first rumble of thunder. The formation of the team. The deep waters of destiny. A young boy named Puck, who took his first breath beneath the surface and never looked back. A quiet cove where dreams and callings first met. An ancient artifact. A quiet war, brewing. The call to dive deeper.

But take heart. Even now, you're standing at the edge of something vast.

The battle you're about to step into is not just fiction. It's rooted in eternal truth. A war between light and darkness. Between deception and unveiling. Between chaos and creation. Heroes rise in every generation, but only some choose to see. Even fewer choose to act.

Team TIDES is no ordinary group. They are the resurgents, guardians, innovators, and warriors forged by conviction but bonded by something stronger than steel. They are unified by truth, character, and the desire to fight for what is right. What began as a spark is now a wave rising. Their technology is inspired by nature but powered by sacrifice. Their courage is drawn from something ancient and true.

The world they move through may be hidden, but it is not imaginary. It's your world too. Just viewed through a different lens. One where the physical and spiritual collide. Where suits echo the design of creation. Where underwater tunnels lead to places man was never meant to reach, unless he was called, unless he was chosen.

You hold in your hands not just a book, but an invitation to a new world.

To awaken. To remember. To rise. For the shadows are thick, but the light is thicker still. And the tides?

They're turning.

Welcome to the mission.

If you've made it this far, you're already on the path. Don't miss the greatest adventure of your life. The quest may begin in these pages or stir within your heart, but the true adventurer knows: the journey begins the moment both start to turn.

Text Copyright 2025 by Joel P. Chanaca
Illustrations Copyright 2025 by Joel P. Chanaca

# Frogman Puck Resurgent:

# Turn of the Tides

## Unveiling of Shadows: A Quest for Truth

All rights reserved. Printed in the USA.

Library of Congress Control Number: 2025922783

### About the Name 'Puck'

"Puck," "Puck-a-rino," and "Pitter-Puck" are affectionate nicknames bestowed by John Chanaca Sr. upon young dreamers and adventurers with boundless creativity, a thirst for exploration, and the courage to step into the unknown. These names, rooted in a cherished family tradition rather than folklore, serve as a call to embrace the spirit of youthful wonder and forge one's heroic journey.

As Scripture reminds us, "You intended to harm me, but God intended it for good to accomplish what is now being done, the saving of many lives" (Genesis 50:20). God has a way of transforming circumstances for His glory, and in this story, "Puck" represents the boundless joy, courage, and purpose found in a life guided by Him.

No part of this book may be reproduced in any written, electronic, recording, or photocopying
without the written permission of the publisher or author.
https://www.mjchanacapublishing.com/

Publisher: MJChanacapublishing LLC,
Family Values Series
ISBN-13: 978-1963416558 Paperback,
ISBN-13: 978-1963416565 Hardcover,
ISBN-13: 978-1963416541 EBOOK

## Thank You for Diving In!

We hope you love exploring Puck's world of adventure, mystery! Now it's your turn to rise with the tides and help us share this story with the world.

✨ Here's how you can make a splash:

📸 Share a picture of you with your copy of the book, your favorite moment, or a scene on social media, and tag us! Use the hashtag #FrogmanPuck to join the community of adventurers.

🌐 Visit us at MJChanacapublishing.com for exclusive content, behind-the-scenes updates, and access to our free downloadable guides.

📫 Sign up for our newsletter to stay updated on Puck's next adventures and receive special offers and surprises!

💪 Join the Team! Become a Launch Team Member and help spread the word. Get early access to exciting news, upcoming releases, and insider perks.

Let's inspire more dreamers, adventurers, and protectors of the deep. Together, we can create waves!

Take the plunge and help Puck's story rise to the surface.

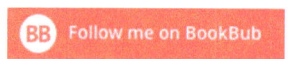

# Chapters

# A New Dawn in the Cove

The gentle swirl of a current outside the underwater porthole shimmered with marine life as the first rays of morning sun pierced the lake's surface. Ripples danced across the observation windows of "The Cove," scattering golden light through the water. The warm touch of sunlight brushed against Puck's eyelids, and he blinked awake. He had rested well in his sleek underwater quarters, a far cry from the rain-speckled living room window he once imagined as a porthole to adventure.

Tad was already up, suit on, floating outside the porthole window, tapping the glass and beckoning Puck to join him for a morning dive. With a stretch and a surge of excitement, Puck activated his nano watch. In an instant, bots swarmed and formed his suit, locking into place.

He connected to Sync and hailed Tad. "Good morning, Tadpole," Puck teased.

Tad laughed. "Ha! If you'd gotten up earlier, you'd have seen the first light streaming into the lake. Head to the Cove pool and hit the switch on the side. I'll be waiting out here."

Puck made his way to the Cove Commons and found the button on the tidepool's edge. The pool slid aside, revealing a frogman portal leading out into the lake.

He plunged in and joined Tad beneath the surface. They glided past the observation dome, their silhouettes cascading across the glass, displaying their frogman outlines. This had been a dream, but now a reality. An octopod alert pinged softly on their heads-up display. Jones's voice chimed in through the comms, "Morning, chaps. Wonder what today's tides will bring?"

Puck chuckled. "Let's start slow and explore the lake. I haven't had my coffee yet; sunshine here had to drag me out of bed."

They glided through crystal-clear waters, marveling at the creatures that came to life in the morning light. This life with Team TIDES was more vivid than any dream, brimming with promise and purpose. Before long, others began syncing in, their presence rippling through the lake as they activated ESAT Mode, poised for the day's challenge.

Dr. E's voice crackled over their comms. "How did everyone settle into their new quarters last night?"

Puck was first to reply, grinning even through the mask. "I couldn't imagine asking for anything more. Dr. E., Thank you for everything."

One by one, the others chimed in with their gratitude. Jones added with a hearty laugh, "A new day's dawned. Time for another round of bacon and a cup of joe!"

Agent Hardee's deep chuckle echoed. "We knew you loved roughing it at campfires, Jones, but you didn't waste any time firing up that outdoor cooking station. We'll have a full breakfast after a brief training session. And yes, Puck and Jones, there is plenty of coffee waiting for you, as promised. Let's all rendezvous in the Vaultrium for a quick cup and a pre-training briefing. TIDES align!"

As the command came through Echo-Sync, a holographic route lit up in each visor display. It felt almost physical, as if their very blood pulsed with unity. It was a picture-perfect moment. Team TIDES in perfect formation, every member moving under the same banner of Truth. Zane soared above the Forge's dome, Austin carved arcs on his hoverboard across the lake's surface, while Puck and Tad zipped just below, bubbles trailing in their wake. Jones was beside them in his sleek octopod. The rest of the team advanced on their chosen vehicles, each path converging toward the Vaultrium. Each member was a vital nerve pulsating with the body in sync.

# Echoes of Arrival

The Vaultrium's docking bay doors opened as Team TIDES was inbound, Echo Sync humming through every suit. Two new profiles flickered to life on the central holo-display and with them, two familiar voices crackled over comms.

"Better late than never, Brox." "Better yet, never leave home without Echo Sync, Ryan! Hey everyone, guess who's catching up to you?" Brox's tone was equal parts relief and triumph. Above them, Zane couldn't resist a quip. "I've got two bogies coming in hot!" At his cue, Ryan and Brox activated Echo Sync Amphibious Mode. Their ID modules displayed full biographical data and commendations. Although nobody here needed reminding of who they were, the display showed up-to-date mission training and completed Synchronium stats. Brox sped along with his sleek single-pilot hovercraft; Ryan swooped down in Flight Mode, jets trailing. "Zane, did I mention I love to fly too?" Ryan called out with a grin.

A third ping echoed through Echo Sync as James' profile materialized on the holo-display. "After Brox and Ryan were free of prior commitments," James began, "we ran them through the Synchronium, every recorded operation, every Echo Sync data packet. They're up to speed and ready to roll."

Agent Hardee stepped forward as everyone arrived in perfect sync. There was a circular arena of greeting with Hardee in the center as the TIDES converged. "Give them a warm welcome. We'll need smaller strike teams at multiple sites and fast! We've got members across the globe waiting to sync, but right now, every hand on deck counts."

The team shared a quiet moment of gratitude, heads bowed in unison and agreement. They thanked God for safe passage, for new allies, and for the fellowship that bound them all. They drifted toward the central café module for coffee and light refreshments-a brief pause before the real work began.

Dr. E tapped her cup to draw everyone's focus. "James has been my right hand from day one, engineering marvels, designing breakthroughs, puzzle-solving beyond measure." As the last coffee cup settled on the table, the Vaultrium, itself, seemed to pulse with purpose. In this nexus of light, data, and shared conviction, each member was more than an individual agent. They were neurons in a living organism, firing in perfect synchrony. Together, they formed a single, fluid nerve center, Team TIDES, inside the body of Truth in motion. Dr. E continued, "We have a full day ahead. First, we'll cross-train on our various constructs and suit-mode outputs. Then we'll head to the hospital to meet the RIPTIDE agent we rescued. Thanks to your swift actions and our HUD-based patient monitoring, we got to him just before a blood clot reached his brain. He's stable now, but this is our chance to show him the stark difference between the lies RIPTIDE peddles and the reality we protect." She gestured to James. "James will lead today's sessions. Not only is he a top engineer, but he is also an athlete, a pilot, a diver, and a tinkerer. James, take it away."

James stood and addressed the team. "You all know our systems are cutting-edge. We've designed them to adapt instantly to whatever environment or threat we face. In a crisis, you can't wait for slow, bureaucratic fixes. That's where the nanobots come in: they analyze, communicate, and adapt in real time to meet your needs. When truth and integrity matter, you need tools that respond as quickly as your convictions do." He paused, letting everything register with them. "Remember, unlike RIPTIDE agents, who twist data, fabricate results, and betray the natural order, we observe nature as it is. We follow God's design for creative development.

"Our strength comes from aligning with Truth, not rewriting it to suit our agenda. That's the alignment in Sync Mode." At James's signal, the Vaultrium's holo-interface flared to life, igniting the training modules in a radiant symphony of light and purpose. Team TIDES stood ready, preparing not just for action but to embody Truth in motion. "Every mission you've logged, dives, rescues, and artifact recoveries, all feed into your suit's adaptive core," James explained. "Our communication highways are engineered like bridges. Information only flows when there's a solid path. Nothing with Echo Sync Amphibious Technology happens by accident." He swept his hand through the glowing interface. "In the field, your suits continue to harvest information the team shares, and it learns. That is intelligent adaptation. Your body was designed with all its components working together, a communication highway."

The display shifted to a wireframe of a human body, its nervous system pulsing with light. "Team TIDES is like a single organism. Every suit, every construct, every one of you is a vital nerve in this body of Truth. Cross-training allows you to step into any role, whether frogman, pilot, engineer, or all construct modes, without hesitation. Stick with your favorite modes, but learning to switch on the fly makes you stronger."

Hands rose to HUDs as visors lit up in unison, a living network, ready to surge with purpose.

"Let's move to our training grounds, the Synchronium, for some hands-on work," James said. Dr. E smiled, "Choppa choppa, Luna. You might as well take your apprentice too," nodding toward Luna, who had quietly snuck into the meeting. Luna stepped out from behind a console and smiled as she joined the team.

# Shifting Gears: The Synchronium

The team made their way down the corridor toward the Synchronium, boots echoing softly against the polished floor. The atmosphere was alive with energy, quiet anticipation pulsing through each step like a heartbeat syncing to purpose. Among them, Luna moved with eager determination. The daughter of Dr. Zayler and his wife, Celeste. She radiated conviction far beyond her years. Her voice rang out confidently as she walked alongside Mr. Hardee.

"I told my parents," she said, "David was just a youth, probably no older than fifteen, when he faced Goliath. He wasn't old enough to be in the army, but God didn't wait for him to grow older. He used him right where he was. RIPTIDE doesn't care how old I am, so why should I sit back and wait? If God is for me, who can stand against me?"

Mr. Hardee gave a small nod of respect. "Your parents didn't make that decision lightly, Luna. But they saw it, your faith isn't just words. It's steady and grounded. It's their faith being tested, too, as they trust the Lord to guide you into this calling. We'll stand beside you. James said you ran him ragged during training last night using nano-suit and construct modes. He couldn't believe your endurance."

"She even beat me in a reflex drill," James added with a grin, catching up beside them. "Let's just say I needed more coffee than usual this morning."

Luna's eyes lit up. "I'm ready to sync with the full team today."

As they entered the Synchronium, the chamber came to life. Massive, curved walls of the training dome flickered with blue light. Dr. E stepped forward, entering parameters into the console. In seconds, the simulation world unfolded: deep lake zones, rolling forest terrain, elevated platforms, rooftops,

...old bridges, and towering structures surrounded by a field of sky. It was a fluid playground of challenge and realism, built to test skill, adaptability, and teamwork.

Constructs began assembling from the design inputs, materializing like living puzzles that were floating, rotating, and unfolding in elegant motion. They shimmered with energy, offering endless ways to train and adapt. James addressed the now assembled team. "Today, each of you will lead a training segment based on your core strength. Whether it's diving, tech, flight, mechanics, or strategy, everyone has something to offer. The goal is simple: learn from one another and lead one another." He smiled slightly. "Becker would've loved to be here, but he's currently... making up for lost time with Mrs. Becker after being held captive at the RIPTIDE base. Tackling that honey-do list, he said, is harder than facing Eclipse or Ironshade. " A few chuckles broke the tension. "He'll join us later today," James continued. "For now, get ready to shift gears. We added more tech last night. Dr. Zayler, Dr. E, Celeste, and Luna began researching expanded outputs across multiple modes. Luna sparked more ideas than expected after her first wall run in RGM. She even developed a new grapple output mode. Think of it like a frog's tongue snatching prey. It is fast, effective for scaling walls, binding limbs, and reaching high ledges with ease."

Luna stepped forward, eyes gleaming with pride as she activated her arm gauntlet. "It's called TENDRIL," she said, pausing to let the acronym settle. "Tactical Extension for Neutralization, Detainment, Retrieval & Integrated Lift." A shimmer of energy danced across her forearm gauntlet as the prototype deployed a flexible, semi-organic tether arcing toward a distant target. It snapped back with precision, binding a training dummy in seconds.

"It's inspired by real-world biology, and it was easy to adapt the shape since we had the elements already. But we've enhanced it with the same patient monitoring system built into Sync Mode. It's sticky, strong, and smart." Ryan let out a low whistle. "Sticky justice. I like it." Luna smiled. "It can restrain threats without injury, reach high ledges in an instant, and even retrieve objects mid-air. It's not just tech, it's purpose in motion." Dr. E nodded. "It's already queued into your suits. We'll train with it today. We'll cover the rest soon. Let's start in Frogman Mode. Puck and Tad...care to give the team a briefing?" Tad and Puck stepped forward with eager grins. "Absolutely, we're on it!" They took turns explaining the science of diving, how ESAT and HRAM offered enhancements far beyond standard equipment, and emphasized the importance of full safety protocols for the gear.

As Puck and Tad explained in detail, the design communication systems stored user input and encoded it using code, much like a blueprint written into DNA. This information was routed to the central HUB in the Vaultrium, activating real-time frogman Sync Modes and storing the data within the frogman mission archive files. In this way, input could generate improved output modes for future missions. Team members tapped into the flow and experienced the uploaded information like living memories. Neural feedback synced across each suit, forming a seamless bridge between experience and execution. James stepped forward. "Puck and Tad, thank you for the frogman briefing. Without input, we can't generate output. This is design communication at its finest. Technology here is modeled after how real-world adaptation is coded and passed down from generation to generation. We're not evolving by accident; we're advancing by intelligent input, shared code, and a clear purpose.

"Now, who's next?" asked Puck.

One by one, each member stepped forward, committed to teamwork, integrity, dedication, and service, and led their instructional session. Whether it was flight tech, mechanical builds, or strategic constructs, every demonstration studied strategy, design elements, and engineering insights into the HUB. Before long, the team was ready.

The training wasn't just preparation; it had become shared knowledge, lived experience, and encoded wisdom. Together, as a team, they ran through suit generations in multiple modes, collaborated on advanced constructs, then launched into personalized simulations reflecting their unique styles. It was more than training; it was a symbol. A living body in motion. Just as the body of Christ is made of many members, each uniquely crafted yet united under one Head. This team, too, had been designed with purpose. They were Team TIDES, and they were ready.

They had shifted gears, literally and figuratively.

Each member had adapted, applied knowledge from their own field, and synthesized it into collective strength. Physics, strategy, tech, biology, and faith all flowed together in perfect harmony under one unified command: Truth-led leadership. James, Dr. E, and Agent Hardee approached the main console. Their presence, together, sent a ripple of anticipation through the team. Lights across the Synchronium dimmed, then pulsed as new simulations loaded in, casting shimmering reflections across the polished floor like waves of future missions. Agent Hardee's voice rang out, firm and anchored in unshakable conviction. "I can't thank you enough for coming together again. What we're building here is bigger than any one person. It's more than environmental recovery, more than pushing back against RIPTIDE..."

He paused, his gaze steady. "This is for all people. God's people."

Even the ones who don't yet realize they need rescuing.

"Our mission will take us into cities, rural towns, island outposts, and even international territories. Not just to stop villains, but to intervene for the innocent. We follow clues embedded in the artifacts we've unearthed, clues left behind so that Truth can be revealed." He tapped the edge of the display, and a simulation loaded: a digital alleyway, cold and shadowed. "We will not stand for injustice, not from RIPTIDE, and not from any force that seeks to harm others. If we can act, but instead remain silent, evil gains ground." His voice lowered but carried weight.

"Ephesians 5:11 reminds us: 'Have nothing to do with the fruitless deeds of darkness, but rather expose them.' That's what we do. We carry the light." Dr. E stepped forward, her voice calm but resolute. "We don't answer to fame or fear. We answer to Truth. That Truth is what makes us more than just defenders." She met the eyes of each team member.

"We are servants and harvest workers."

Hardee turned back to the display. "Your first trial scenario: a dangerous fugitive has escaped custody. He's broken into a home, stolen funds, and is now armed on foot, navigating an urban alleyway. He poses a real threat to innocent lives." His gaze swept the room. "Your mission is not to destroy, it's to de-escalate. Apprehend with the least force necessary. We are not vigilantes. We are a covert, sanctioned branch tasked with delivering justice and preserving life." He paused. "You bring him down. You bring him in. Are you ready?" All but their heartbeats, the room was silent. Then, in unison, visors locked into place. HUDs lit up. Sync linked them in a synchronized flash. They were more than ready.

15

# Forged in Fire

The holo-walls around Puck, Tad, and James melted into a living replica of the invaded home. Dim light flickered through digital windows; scattered toys lay on the floor of the family room. Puck crouched beside a holographic family silhouette, tracing the last known movements. Tad scanned the shattered doorframe, finger-painting the entry point in mid-air. James tapped his gauntlet, pulling up overlays of stolen items, weapon types, and suspect apparel data streaming in real-time to the central HUB. When the intel feed synced, they deployed micro-drones from their suits that drifted into the street, linking to local police radios and satellite arrays. Facial-recognition algorithms locked onto a signature behind a dumpster in the alley, and their HUDs pulsed green with a target lock. "Let's move," Puck murmured. Instantly, they summoned their hoverboard constructs. They glided effortlessly towards the target. Nearing the scene, James's projection module flared: a perfect decoy to walk toward the escaped convict. In one fluid motion, he walked past the target and positioned himself on his flank, completely unseen. Puck triggered Frogman Mode and arced a TENDRIL to a balcony above the suspect. His stance radiated fluid precision, knees bent, forearms leveled, eyes locked.
For a breathless second, he hovered in silence, like justice held in tension, waiting to strike.
Tad engaged RGM (HRAM), anchoring him against the opposite wall as he hung in shadow, ready to spring. The suspect emerged, engaging James' decoy, knife gleaming in the dim alley light. The suspect moved in, engaging the decoy.
Puck's voice crackled over comms:
"We've confirmed ID. Move in when you're ready, minimum force."

16

A heartbeat later, Puck flicked his wrist and launched TENDRIL, a sticky mesh-like grappling that whipped through the air like a living tongue, wrapping the knife hilt in a sticky embrace. Puck snatched the blade from his grasp. Tad activated his ink cloud, and a thick, harmless mist billowed around the suspect, disorienting him. Meanwhile, James terminated the decoy projection and, at the same time, shot a sticky goo net around the subject. Within seconds, the suspect was disarmed and immobilized. The trio stepped back as "OPERATION SUCCESS" glowed across each HUD, and the next group readied themselves.

Luna, Brox, and Ryan entered the chamber, and the simulation shifted to a fog-shrouded harbor inlet at dawn. Ships bobbed against the docks, and cranes loomed like silent sentinels above the water. The scenario portrayed a harbormaster held at bay by a suspect brandishing a stun baton. Luna slipped into RGM and pressed her sticky boots and gloves to the ship's steel hull, crawling upward in near silence to peer through a pilot-house window. Ryan transitioned from Frogman to Flight Mode and ascended overhead for an aerial sweep. On the quay, Brox entered Stealth Mode, his ANV (Amphibious Night Vision) thermal vision scanning for heat signatures.

Luna's voice crackled over comms. "Raised voices near the pilot house." Ryan deployed a drone to circle the opposite side and gain another angle. Brox unleashed a TENDRIL that darted across the gap, wrapping around a cleat to hoist him aboard. Ryan generated a hologram distraction to draw out their opponent. The suspect spun at the sudden movement just as Ryan's holographic decoy dashed across the deck.

Seizing the moment, Luna unleashed a precise blast of nano-pulse sonic energy from her forearm module. The stun baton vibrated fiercely, sparks dancing as it clattered to the deck. Brox followed instantly, launching a second TENDRIL that wrapped the suspect's legs like a fast-moving vine, pulling him gently off balance without harm. Ryan dropped in beside them, hovering before he touched down, quickly transitioning to Frogman Mode, and applied a final strand of nano-tether across the suspect's arms to complete the restraint.

In seconds, the harbormaster was safe, and the perpetrator immobilized. The simulation froze, casting a soft glow across their visors as the words "HOSTAGE SAFE" were confirmed across each HUD.

Exhilarated, the trio exited the simulation chamber, exchanging high-fives and encouragement as the next group suited up. Austin, Jones, and Zane took their turn next, applying everything they'd learned in their unique blend of humor, grit, and growth. Derrick, Jordan, and Agent Hardee paired off as well, running advanced modules focused on coordinated strategy and rapid-response maneuvers. Throughout each session, the Sync link enabled more than just real-time collaboration; it fostered something deeper: mutual understanding.

They trained until the system marked the cycles complete, and the final simulation faded. The team returned to their quarters, each member emerging freshly showered and reset, eventually gathering in the commons for a well-earned meal. The room buzzed with light teasing and laughter, like siblings around a family table. Stories from their simulations flew around between bites of food, and even the newest members felt like they'd been there since the beginning.

There were different personalities, skill sets, and life paths, yet somehow, it all fit. What once felt like a patchwork of individuals had become something far more intricate and beautiful. They had learned each other's rhythms in Sync, but more than that, they had learned to value the unique gift each person brought to the mission. It wasn't about uniformity; it was about family. This wasn't just training. It was a fellowship. They weren't merely superheroes shaped by nanotech and strategy; they were believers, living out the very truths they defended. Warriors who didn't fight for glory, but for grace. They weren't just here to be guardians; they were here to love one another. To lift the fallen. To forgive the broken, even those who had once stood on the wrong side of the fight.

Puck glanced around the table, the laughter and camaraderie still echoing in his ears, and something settled in his chest. A realization deeper than anything he'd felt in the heat of battle.

The team had grown, both in numbers and with purpose. Each person, uniquely designed, bore a spark of the Creator's intentionality. Each one had a calling. None was more important than the other. Their strength wasn't found in power or performance, but in who they were becoming together. Agent Hardee stepped forward, his tone calm but purposeful. "We've accomplished a lot this morning," he said, scanning their faces, "but we're not done yet. It's time to head to the hospital. We've got a meeting with the RIPTIDE agent, and we need to see where this thread leads." Puck nodded, a quiet resolve in his voice. "We've come this far. Let's see how far we can take this." With the entire team's agreement, they suited back up and loaded into Jordan's massive, armored mobile command center.

# Out of the Shadows: First Light

As the engines hummed to life and the vehicle rumbled down the road, there was a feeling in the air. It wasn't tension, not fear. It was mission-focused.

On the edge of the harbor bay, they pulled into the hospital compound with a surge of anticipation. This wasn't just any hospital; it was part of their own secure network, funded by the same covert branch that supported Team TIDES.

Agent Hardee opened the door as they exited. "As I've mentioned, we have allies in every sector," he said, leading them through the gated entrance. "Our funding came from numerous partnerships and credible government leadership. However, some'd like to see us fail. Some, who crave access to our resources for their own gain."

He paused, eyes sweeping the secure perimeter. "This facility is fortified, but we suspect there are moles planted within the agency. That's probably how RIPTIDE located Dr. E's symbiotic prototype. Stay vigilant. Be careful who you trust. Wolves in sheep's clothing wear many faces."

Austin grinned. "Top secret mission stuff, got it."

The group laughed, and Tad quipped, "Only you, Austin, only you!"

They made their way to the reception desk, where Dr. E produced a stack of badges. "Almost forgot your ID badges," she said, handing one to each team member. "They'll open doors today, and in the days to come."

Austin hung his badge around his neck and saluted theatrically. "See? Top secret mission stuff. I love it."

The others smiled, the gravity of the moment tempered by their growing camaraderie. With badges secured and purpose in their hearts, Team TIDES stepped into the lobby, ready to confront the next chapter of Truth.

The team filed down the hushed corridor toward the hospital wing. Dr. E leaned in and whispered, "His name is Sinclair." Agent Hardee gave a curt nod to the guard, who pushed open the heavy door. Stepping inside, Hardee placed a reassuring hand on Puck's shoulder and said, "Sinclair asked for you two specifically. Lead the conversation. We're here for support." Puck and Tad exchanged a brief look and advanced into the room. There, resting near the far wall, was Sinclair. He was hooked to monitoring equipment but steady-eyed.

"There you are," he said, voice rough but sincere. "I've wanted to see you face-to-face. I hear I nearly died. A blood clot was racing to my brain. The doctors caught it just in time. But I can't reconcile the rage I was taught to feel with what I see before me. You, Team TIDES, should be my natural enemies. Yet something in me won't let me hate you. At least, not anymore."

He paused, gathering his thoughts. "All that anger, the contempt, the disgust, they're gone and replaced by... something I can't name. I feel compassion, respect, and even hope. It's confusing because I used to think feelings were weakness." Sinclair's eyes flicked to Puck and back. "Now, instead of wishing you'd fail, I find myself rooting for your success. I want nothing to do with my past. I don't understand what you did. Was it in that tranquilizer dart? A secret drug? A mind-altering agent?"

His gaze held theirs, searching. "Please, tell me. What is happening to me?" Puck offered his hand first, then Tad, and finally introduced each member of the team. He turned back to Sinclair. "Mr. Sinclair, we're not here to disrupt you, but to confront the actions, decisions, and direction RIPTIDE has chosen. We fight for Truth and light, and for the well-being of all God's people."

24

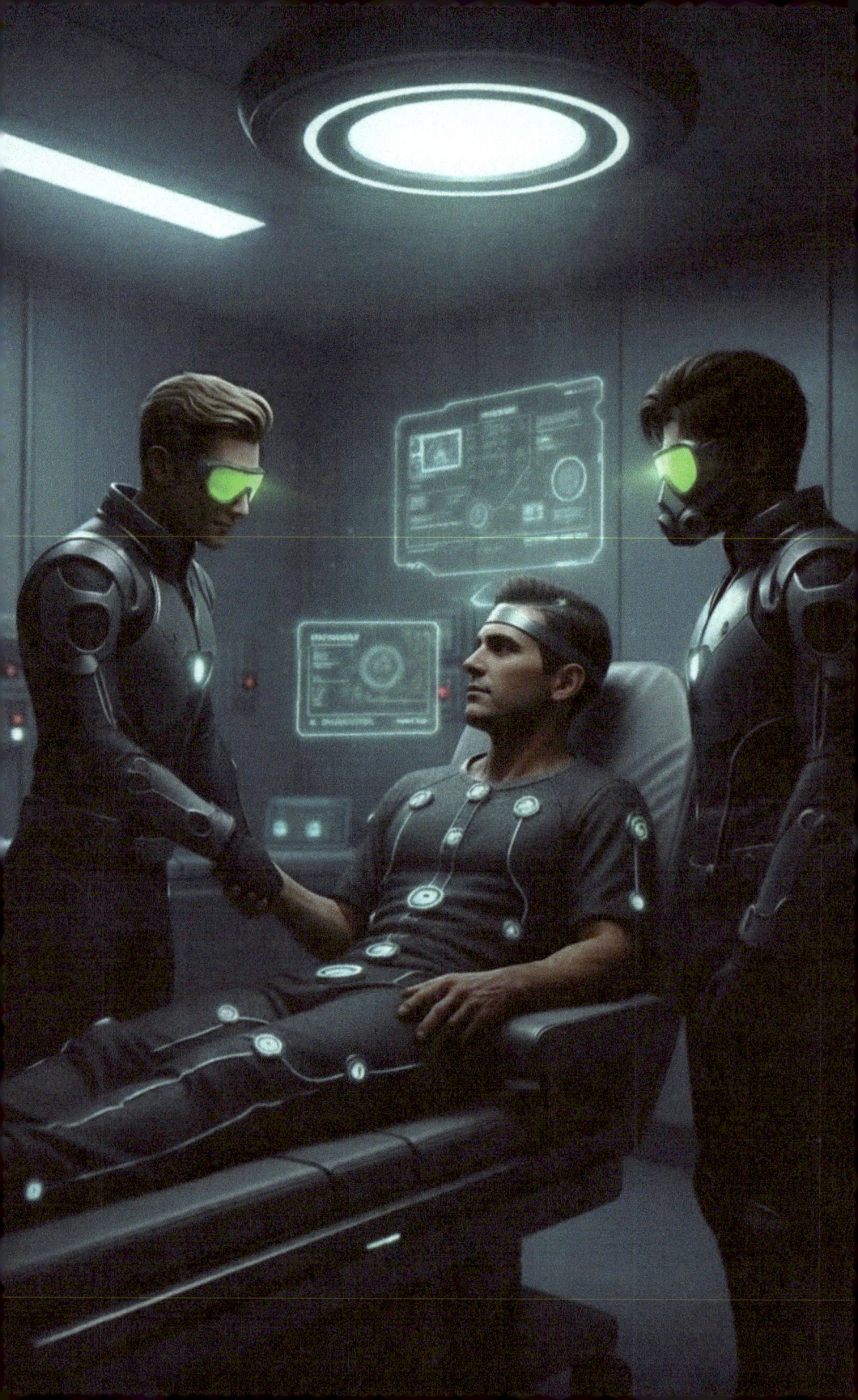

Puck retracted his face mask and leaned in, his voice steady but full of compassion. "What you're experiencing is clarity. It may be just for a moment, but it's enough to make a choice. We've all been given free will from the beginning, from our Father. What you're feeling now isn't manipulation or confusion; it's the Holy Spirit. He's opening your eyes. Letting you feel compassion. Redemption. You let your guard down when kindness was shown to you. What you received wasn't weakness. It was grace.

You were helped by people who follow God's Truth. Not because we or you deserve it, but because He loves us, right where we are, in the middle of our mess. In the middle of our sin. And yet, He came. He lived. He died. And He rose again. That act of grace, through Christ's work on the cross, offers you the greatest gift, eternal life. And when you receive that, it changes everything: the way you see the world, and the way you live in it. You can yield to the Holy Spirit drawing you, or reject Him, and return to the old way. That's your choice. He will eternally honor either decision you make. But I urge you, yield now. You don't know if you'll get this moment again." Sinclair's expression tightened, memories rising to the surface. "Most of RIPTIDE isn't unaware of God's existence. In fact... they reject Him with everything they've got.

Some agents deny His power. Others deny He exists at all. They tell us He's abandoned this world and that we're on our own. It's every man for himself. The more we take now, the more we follow our own desires, the more we fill our pockets with easy money, the less we have to think about Him. RIPTIDE teaches us to be secretive. To bend facts. Shape the story. Rewrite the narrative to suit our needs. If there's truth in the world, we bury it. And if there's a lie that advances our goals, we broadcast it like it's the truth.

26

"They say we're the most evolved beings on the planet. That we bow to no one and we are wise," Sinclair continued, his voice low. "RIPTIDE, they truly believe they're smarter than you... smarter than anyone who believes in admitting fault." He paused, looking at both Puck and Tad. "I would've died back at that RIPTIDE base. I know that now. If you hadn't come when you did, if I had gotten the drop on you instead of you getting the drop on me, I wouldn't be here. I've been thinking about everything before that encounter, about the person I let myself become. I hate what they turned me into. I let them shape me with lies... and believe our own lies. The more we repeated them, the more we believed them. I feel dirty from it. And the strange thing is, if I hadn't realized I was sick through my own defeat, if I had succeeded, if I had just carried on, I'd probably be dead by now. But instead, this illness —and that failure —it feels like a second chance. Like a doorway cracked open."

His voice cracked slightly. "I want out. I want to change. I want to be free of this. What do I have to do to be rid of it for good?"

Tad leaned forward, eyes steady. "You didn't know you were sick, physically, mentally, or spiritually. But the moment you recognized you had a second chance and asked, you found the answer. People who think they're fine never ask for a lifeline. They are set in their ways, heels dug in, and think they have grounds to explain their viewpoint the the Great I Am, after it is too late.

The truth is, we've all broken God's law. Maybe it seems small, stealing something insignificant, telling a 'white lie,' trusting something more than God, but it matters. His law is written on our hearts. Deep down, we know we don't measure up. We know we need a Savior.

That guilt or fear you feel? It's a signpost to turn around. Without it, we convince ourselves we're 'good enough,' and that God owes us grace. But that's pride. That's self-righteousness. It's the same flaw that destroyed our true enemy.

We broke the law. But Jesus paid the debt. He offers forgiveness, not because we earned it, but because He loved us enough to die in our place. That's the Gospel. And like any gift, you can't receive it unless you reach out and accept it." Puck stepped beside him, speaking with gentle confidence. "If you believe in your heart and confess with your mouth that Jesus Christ is Lord, that He lived, died, and rose again. You will be saved. Admit that you've sinned. That you've fallen short. And ask Him to forgive you. Turn from sin and towards Christ. From that moment on, everything changes.

Sin won't sit right with you anymore. Even if you stumble, you'll feel it immediately, like being out of step with someone you are walking with. You'll want to make it right. This isn't religion. It's a relationship. You'll walk with Him. Let Him teach you, lead you, and speak to you, just like He's doing right now. It might not make sense to others, but to your spirit... it'll be undeniable."

Without hesitation, Sinclair bowed his head and spoke with trembling honesty. "I know this is the Truth. I believe Jesus died for me... and rose again. I need You, God. Forgive me. Clean me. I turn from sin and from who I was. I want to live for you. I surrender to you and put my trust in you alone."

In that moment, the man who once served darkness was gone. A new creation stood in his place. Born again by the Spirit of God. The old passed, and everything became new. He had stepped out of the shadows and into the light for the first time. The room seemed to glow with quiet wonder.

The presence of the Lord was unmistakable, and every heart in the room felt it. Sinclair looked up, eyes wet but steady, and turned to Agent Hardee. "You seem like a man who gets things done. How does someone... completely display change? I already sense the difference. But I want that change to be visible too, not just to honor you rendering aid, but to honor God... for saving me."

Hardee smiled. "We can handle that. That sense you feel is confirmation. Skeptics could never understand what it is until they yield. It is all about where you place your trust. You'll be cleared through medical shortly. And if you're ready, we can baptize you as a public declaration of your new faith." Sinclair nodded slowly. "Yes. That would mean everything to me." He hesitated, then added, "There's one more thing. I don't want to be called Sinclair anymore. That name belonged to someone else, someone who lived in the shadows. I want something that reflects who I am now." He looked at the team, eyes searching. "There's a story in the Bible about a man who ran from God and was swallowed by a great fish. He spent three days in the dark, but God didn't give up on him. When he finally surrendered, he was spit out as a free man. Jonah, right? How about... Jonah Freeman?"

Mr. Hardee nodded to Dr. E, who silently pulled out her handheld device. Her fingers moved swiftly, wiping every trace of the old file. A new profile appeared.

Hardee rested a hand on his shoulder. "Normally, people answer for their actions. But today... God has set you free. And we're going to honor that." He glanced around the room, then back at Jonah. "In law enforcement, we sometimes turn criminals into informants. Not because they're innocent, but because they're valuable and willing to do what's right. We could use you on the team if you'll join us."

Jonah looked around the room, locking eyes with each member of the team. A fire had lit behind his eyes, not of anger, but of purpose. "I couldn't imagine what else I would do. Where would I even go? Who could I trust? I have so much to learn... and even more to give. I've spent years taking. I want to give back now. If even one person could experience this first breath of real life, I have to be part of that." Hardee nodded. "Very well. We'll use your insight. You can't fight an enemy you don't understand. You've seen the inside of their system. You know their strategies. You are part of the family now." Just then, the attending physician walked in, "Agent Hardee, always a pleasure." Hardee gave the nod and acknowledged him, "Dr. Christenson." The doctor scanned the holographic chart. "Vitals are strong. The presence in the room is strong, too. Glad you yielded, Sinclair," Dr. Christenson said, with a knowing grin. "It's Jonah Freeman now, and thank you, Dr. Christenson. " Dr. Christenson nodded, "You are quite welcome."

While the staff began packing up the equipment and preparing the release paperwork, Brox and Ryan lingered at the edge of the room, quiet and observant. A flicker of movement caught Brox's eye. An orderly halfway down the hallway had paused at the corner. He raised a phone, snapped a photo of the room, and quickly ducked out of sight. A moment later, Ryan saw him texting, back turned, glancing nervously toward the corridor camera. They exchanged a silent look, instincts on high alert. "That wasn't right," Ryan muttered, already moving. They notified the team, and within moments, Dr. E and James had quietly flagged the hospital's internal personnel system. After a brief, hushed conversation, he identified the orderly, "Corbin Vale," as a recent referral, transferred in by a politician, a senator. Senator Emory Slate.

Hardee's eyes narrowed. "A favor from a senator," he said under his breath. "We need to trace that thread. And fast."

James and Dr. E were already moving, fingers dancing across their wrist consoles as encrypted access points opened. Internal logs, clearance histories, digital footprints-data flowed like current from a frayed wire.

Brox kept his eyes on Jonah, who stood tall for the first time. He looked lighter, like a man who'd just walked out of a dark prison and into the first light of day.

His new life had only just begun... and already, the shadows stirred.

Hardee clapped his hands once, sharp and clear.

"Let's go. We've got a baptism to get to, and we'll deal with moles and whatever this is afterwards. Right now, this moment is about life. About truth. And about making the enemy watch what they can't counterfeit."

A few minutes later...

The team emerged into sunlight at the lake near the center of the compound, calm waters rimmed by trees, the breeze still and reverent. Members of the medical staff and tech division had followed quietly, drawn by the shift in Jonah's countenance. They weren't just curious. They were witnesses.

They waded into the lake. Their suits shimmered in the sunlight, then flickered; nanobots swarmed around them and retracted, folding back into their sync-tech watches. It was a moment that didn't need high-tech shells, but heart.

Jonah stepped forward in a hospital gown. No hesitation. No fear. Just a purpose. Puck turned to him. "What's about to happen is a symbol of what's already happened inside you. The old Sinclair was buried with Christ. The new creation was raised to walk in the light with the risen Christ."

Jonah nodded, emotion tightening his jaw.

They lowered him into the water.
Dead to the past.
They raised him up.
Alive in Christ.
The Breath of Life.

"Jonah," Puck continued, his voice steady and resonant, "this is more than a name change, it's a portrait of real transformation. A seed is buried, appearing lifeless. Yet when combined with water and sunlight, it sprouts, grows, bears fruit, supports life, and renews creation. That's the parable of Christ, buried, risen, and multiplied through God's design." He paused, letting the metaphor settle. "Your name is fitting. Jesus was the seed who died, was buried, and rose again. The Bible naturally and spiritually connects this. When skeptics asked for a sign, Jesus pointed to Jonah's story, buried, delivered, and sent onward. It's a sign we can't ignore." Puck's tone softened, urgent and intimate. "We live in days when many resemble those before the flood or at Babel, pursuing their desires and forgetting the Creator. But here we stand, witnesses to God's work in you. Today, heaven rejoices."

A hush fell over the gathering. A hospital staff member gently handed Jonah a towel. Tad clapped him firmly on the back. Zane leaned in and said, "Welcome home." One by one, Austin, Jordan, Derrick, Jones, Matt, Brox, James, Dr. E, Hardee, Luna, Ryan, and Tad approached to congratulate him. The lake's surface glimmered with reflected sunlight and sky. In that moment, the world felt aligned. The seed had been planted, the light had broken through, and the light would nourish the growth. This was the primary objective and the Great Commission, the entire purpose of doing your part. But Peace never lingers long in a battle zone.

# A Quest of Truth

As the team returned to the common room, drying off and settling in, they gathered in a moment of thanksgiving for their new brother. Each member thanked God for keeping them safe, strengthening them for the mission, and bringing Jonah into their lives.

"Now I understand why you've been so passionate about stewardship and faith," Jonah breathed, eyes bright. "I was blind, living on lies and half-truths. But now, I feel God's presence in every breath. I see the world differently. If RIPTIDE's falsehoods had their way, I'd still be trapped in darkness. They don't see the light... and they won't stop."

At that moment, the wall-mounted screen buzzed to life with an urgent alert. Every head snapped up.

"BREAKING NEWS," the headline blared, its tone clipped, accusatory.

A grainy loop of Team TIDES in action played on a jagged loop. Voices overlapped:

"A misguided, unauthorized group... disrupting production... interfering with legal commerce... targeting private facilities under the guise of environmental defense."

The footage shifted to shaky clips of drilling rigs and labs.

"Internal sources say this rogue outfit halted Shell Corp's environmental project, dangerous, they claim, yet independent experts stand by the data and insist the operation was legal."

The room held its breath.

Jonah's jaw clenched. "Classic RIPTIDE smear, twisting the truth to hide their own misdeeds." Hardee stepped forward, voice low and steady. "They're scrambling to control the narrative, poisoning public opinion before anyone sees the real story." James leaned in. "If they're pushing this hard... they're scared."

Dr. E tapped her wrist. "I traced the feed's origin. It wasn't a leak, it was injected from an encrypted node tied to a lobbyist group linked with..."

"...Senator Emory Slate," Hardee finished.

Puck's gaze went steel-bright. "Then maybe it's time we follow Ephesians 5:11 to the letter."

They lowered their voices as the hologram vanished.

"Who owns the group?" Puck asked Dr. E.

"Guess," she replied.

"Slate," Hardee confirmed. "The same man who twice voted to strip our funding and called us a rogue militia."

Puck stepped forward. "We won't compromise sensitive intel, but we expose the darkness, operate in truth, and let the world see it. If Slate and his mole are smearing us, there must be other senators, leaders, citizens who'll stand for truth once they see it."

Hardee nodded. "If this smear gains traction, good senators will get calls. They'll have to choose, stand with us, or fold." His watch buzzed. "Emergency oversight hearing, the Senate wants me now. I've got to go."

Dr. E squared her shoulders. "I'll return to the Forge and coordinate from the Vaultrium. Prep intel logs, mission data, personnel files, anything we need if things go sideways."

Puck looked to her. "Record the next mission from our POV-high-def, full overlay. Don't release it yet, but be ready."

"We'll have it ready," she said, tapping her device.

A soft chime pulsed on every watch. They tapped in unison, and a 3D overlay flared between them, issuing the call that would send most of the team racing north.

PRIORITY MISSION ALERT – LIVE FEED
Location: Baffin Bay, Greenlandic Shelf
Violation: Unauthorized marine disruption
Threat Level: HIGH – Possible RIPTIDE involvement
Details: Vessel observed; illegal whale-poaching using
cloaked sonar nets. From: the Vaultrium, Dr. Zayler, and
Celste. Source: Satellite feed.

Puck studied the read-out. "Our first real call-out, this can't
be a coincidence." "Wait," Brox said, stepping forward.
"They're dividing us. They are pulling Hardee out to distract
us." Ryan nodded. "We are united in sync. We stay. We track
the mole here, blend in, and feed intel back."
Without hesitation, they activated their disguise protocols.
Their suits rippled and reshaped them into two unremarkable
hospital orderlies, each clutching a clipboard.
Brox smirked. "We'll know what flavor gum he chews by
sundown." "Good," Hardee said, eyeing them. "Keep quiet.
Don't let him slip away." Jonah, fresh from baptism and still
wrapped in a towel, stepped forward. "RIPTIDE never acts at
random. If that orderly saw me, they'd spin this exact
distraction. They're trying to shade, confuse, and divide us."
"Come with us," Jordan said quietly. "You're heading back to
the Forge to help coordinate from there."
Dr. E, Jonah, Jones, Derrick, and Jordan slipped out together,
one group to rebuild and reinforce. Hardee paused at the
doorway, his suit transitioned into Flight Mode.
"God be with you all. Let's show them who we are, and don't
forget your families. They need to know the truth, too."
Everyone engaged Echo-Sync Huds and stayed locked in the
flow. The team engaged in full sync as a unit. Then he was
gone.

Above them, the sky rippled as the remaining team members activated Flight Mode: Tad, Zane, Luna, Austin, James, Matt, and Puck. In moments, they hovered in formation, nanotech thrusters humming.

"Baffin Bay," Luna said, visor locked on target. "They won't see us coming."

Tad grinned. "But they'll know when we arrive."

"Let's move," Puck ordered. With a silent rip of propulsion, Team TIDES vaulted north, leaving the hospital behind for ice and sea. Once at altitude, they monitored real-time weather patterns, air traffic patterns, thermal scans, and sonar overlays weaving through their visors.

Hardee's calm voice crackled in their ears: "I'll feed you hearing updates as they happen."

Then, in unison, they initiated the family link, calling home in a secure conference. One by one, each spoke the truths that bound them: RIPTIDE's web of lies; the living acronym TIDES-Teamwork, Integrity, Dedication, Excellence, Service; their mission to defend God's creation and wage spiritual warfare under the Great Commission. They shared Jonah's journey from darkness into light, the twin armors they now bore nanotech and faith, shield and sword.

Questions melted into affirmations. Promises to pray, to support, to stand firm swelled into a chorus of love. In that sacred moment, distance vanished, and their families became a spiritual fortress around them. Each call was an empowering moment, adding strength to the team.

Then Matt's turn came. He caught his wife's smile across the call. "Meet me at the marina," she said. They'd prayed over selling the ship store, and now the sale was final, God's confirmation on their hearts. Though the decision terrified them, he and his wife felt called to move to an island, restore old vessels back to sea-worthy fishing boats and plant a church in the community. Eric, Jordan's brother and his business partner, Tommy, would take the helm of the marina, weaving ties to the Old Blackwater River: history etched on the walls, artifacts whispering stories, and even a train-restoration exhibit to revive downtown's heritage. They recruited Alex, a seasoned shipmaster, to chart the course for this living museum on the water. Hardee had already blessed Matt's calling and arranged for a nearby TIDES "pod" to keep them in fellowship. Matt's heart raced as he spoke into his comm. "I've felt a tug on my soul. Just like the fishermen in Galilee when Jesus called them to leave their nets. I can't ignore this pull." He looked skyward, then back at the team. "Pray for me as I step out in faith." His voice wavered with joy and sorrow. "I'll be there as soon as I can. See you soon." With that, he peeled off formation, tilting south toward the new destiny God had set before him. This was not goodbye but proof that the body of Christ can stretch across every shore. It isn't always about our comfort; often, the greatest adventures require a leap of faith. Puck watched Matt's silhouette fade into the sunset and felt the truth settle in his heart. He remembered when Tad moved away from Starlight Cove. Loneliness drove him into service, helping his parents and apprenticing with Matt at the marina. That extra time unearthed more than chores; it led him to a dusty bottle in the attic, the first clue of an epic quest. Even Tad's departure, once a stab to Puck's chest, had prepared him for this moment. Now, flanked by Tad in Flight Mode and Zane soaring alongside, Puck saw how far they'd come. Would any of this have happened if Tad's dad hadn't taken the job in the other town? In that instant, he knew: God is in control, and those who trust Him chart new courses through every change.

As the sky glowed like a lighthouse beam, he recalled the riddle's promise-
"The light of space stands tall in its place,
Rooted on earth, below the hands that trace,
The flow of time to guide the vessel,
That bears the weight of what truly matters.
Take with you what you have discovered,
For only together will the truth be uncovered."
-guiding their next voyage toward the hidden artifacts yet to be found.

He thought of early mariners, eyes on sails and stars, trusting unseen winds to steer ancient hulls across vast seas. The rudder obeys the helm, but the ship moves only when unseen wind fills its canvas, its force invisible yet unmistakable in its power. So it is with faith and the Holy Spirit, breathed into us, guiding our course even when we cannot see the path ahead.

Memories surfaced: Tad's painful departure, Matt's faithful service at the marina, Zane filling the space in Tad's absence. That all came after a sharp change. Yet those who are blinded by their belief in random events call this narrow-mindedness. The Truth is, it's clarity and sharp focus. It was like the lens of the bottle holding the path ahead, but it was only visible when the light shone through its surface. It was a leading of the Spirit and making things clear to those who seek Him. Now, aloft in Flight Mode, Puck felt that same Spirit lifting him beyond fear. The riddle, their mission, and this promise of light settled into his soul: they would navigate by God's unseen wind, together uncovering every truth. He exhaled, resolve sharpening like a compass needle. It was time to focus on the quest: study their opponent, refine their strategy, and trust God's timing for every turn in the tide.

# Unveiling of Shadows

The Arctic horizon yawned before their eyes. A frozen frontier alive with hidden danger. Beneath the ice, the faint echoes of a trapped giant drew them onward. Puck glanced at his teammates, resolve burning in their Sync Mode streams.

"All right," he murmured, voice low and certain. "We carry the light and we'll show the world why it matters. In, out, safe. Lord, guide our speed and precision."

With that, they plunged further into the polar sky, a beacon of truth racing to meet the shadows below.

Back at the Forge's Vaultrium, the command center hummed with life. Jordan and Dr. E took their places beside Dr. Zayler and Celeste around the interactive Halo Hub. Derrick, Jones, and Jonah went to the adjacent comms tower. They tapped into three live feeds, documenting and recording everything: the sea team's advance, Brox and Ryan's covert hospital surveillance, and Hardee's hearing. Though some went in opposite directions, their mission was singular. They were meant to expose the works of darkness and let Truth shine.

In the hospital's silent corridors, Brox and Ryan blended into the staff. Their comms crackled to life. "We've locked onto the mole," Brox reported in a hush. "Micro-bot deployed, tracking every step." "Audio's clear," Ryan whispered. "He's feeding someone details through an earpiece."

On the Hub's main screen, a micro-drone scuttled down a wall, slipped onto the orderly's sleeve, then crawled to his shoulder. The hospital's fluorescent lights glinted off its chrome shell with only a pinprick of light. The audio feed picked up a low voice:

"Did it work? What happened after the broadcast?"

"Hardee's on his way to the hearing," the mole hissed. "The rest of Team TIDES just walked out of the building."

Derrick leaned close to Jonah and Jones. "We've got it, recording live audio and video now."
In the Vaultrium, Dr. E, Jordan, Dr. Zayler, and Celeste watched as the feeds ignited across the central display. Satellite overlays traced the sea team's progress toward the pack ice, while a window in the corner flickered with live footage from Hardee's Senate hearing.

Puck's voice cut through the comms with steady authority: "Keep me posted. Team, move fast. We have one shot at this."
All around the Forge, faith and technology fused into an unbreakable force, ready to pierce the darkest lies with blazing truth. The Halo Hub's walls pulsed with data. Thermal scans of the Arctic, encrypted hospital audio, and live video from the hearing stream were another piece of the puzzle they were determined to solve.

Outside the Forge, in the hidden corridors of the hospital, Brox and Ryan monitored the orderly's movements. With their micro-bot secure, they slipped away to speak with Jonah's doctor and gather anything useful about the mole's behavior. In a small, private office, the doctor stood and extended a hand. "I'm Dr. Christenson," he said. "Agent Hardee and I go way back as childhood friends, same church, and countless fishing trips. He always dreamed of serving the public, leading by example. I found my calling in medicine, helping people and caring for injured wildlife. We've both tried to give back, because we've been so blessed."
He glanced toward the hallway before continuing. "The orderly acting strange today, he's only been here a few months. An unusual case. Came through a different channel than normal, but he was signed off... quickly."

"The senator," Ryan muttered, eyes narrowing, "providing slick access for his spy." Dr. Christenson nodded grimly. "Vale's smooth on paper, fast-tracked by some shadow-level clearance... but this leak, if it runs deep, he can't be alone. His arrival was before Becker's capture."

Before anyone could respond, the comms flared to life. The micro-bot's feed picked up again, sharp and clear. "Hello?" Vale's voice answered low, cautious. A second voice came through, clipped and professional, unnervingly familiar, "Hardee is inside. The hearing just opened. The team should be split up by now. Their leader's distraction buys us time. Are we in the clear?" the voice asked. "I think so," Corbin Vale whispered. "They were so focused on Sinclair, they barely noticed me. Took him out back. Dunked him in a lake or something, I have no clue what that was about." A pause. "That's... strange," the voice replied. "Could be one of their rituals. Team TIDES is known for its odd faith-based practices. Possibly symbolic. Water always means something."

From his position in the comm tower, Brox's voice came over the channel, tight and direct. "Hardee, are you getting this? The other voice... It's with you. Somewhere close."

Hardee shifted in his seat at the hearing, eyes moving slowly across the crowd. He leaned and whispered, "Looking now. Micro-bot has a signal lock that traces audio to its source. Stand by... I've got it. Uploading image to Vaultrium now." At the Forge, inside the Valtrium, Dr. E responded instantly. "Got it. Running facial recognition, stand by... Confirmed. You're not going to believe this." A moment passed. Then:

"It's Desmond Vale. Emory Slate's senior aide and nephew. Corbin's cousin. This just cracked wide open." Hardee's jaw tightened. "Of course. Desmond's been claiming the budget's bloated.

47

He is always pushing for privatized 'eco-defense alternatives' that redirect funds to shell companies. Turns out, those companies are all run by Slate's allies and donors."

Ryan's voice came in low over the channel, full of grit. "So, the senator installs his own blood as a mole... and his golden boy is whispering poison in the ears of policy makers. They wanted us to split. Distracted. Burned." Brox added, "Classic misdirection. If you can't prove your own position, smear your opponent and change the focus while sculpting a narrative."

In the Vaultrium, Dr. E looked up from her station. "We're weaving the net. Threads are connecting. We have comm logs, facial ID, and digital trails. Let's keep an eye on both Vales and document everything." Jordan stood beside her, expression cold and focused. "We may have just uncovered the heart of RIPTIDE's misinformation machine." James keyed his mic. "Hardee, I know they are probably making a case against us, but try to keep an eye on Desmond. They're afraid of us and desperate." Dr. Zayler added from the console, "Then we press forward, carefully but deliberately. Truth doesn't hide. But shadows do. Everyone keep at it. This is a quest for Truth."

"I have to go. They are starting, and Slate is bringing the inquiry against us. Don't worry. This ought to be kind of interesting," Hardee whispered.

Deep in the Arctic horizon, their HUDs locked onto a hulking metal vessel, its deck swathed in sonar nets and bristling with harpoons. On a nearby iceberg, Team TIDES touched down. The iceberg's surface cracked softly under their boots.

Inside the Vaultrium, Dr. E's voice relayed over comms. "Satellite confirms your position. I'm scanning beneath the surface, heavy activity below." Puck studied the live feeds, voice calm and precise. "We need eyes everywhere: surface, underwater, and interior." "Luna and I have the surface," James replied, his tone crisp with focus. "Austin and Zane, get on the hull," Puck directed. "On it," Zane answered, eyes narrowing against the whip of wind. Tad stepped forward, activating thermal-solar HRAM. "Puck, we'll take the water."

## On the Surface

Above, Luna and James flicked their wrists to summon hoverboards. They glided above the frigid ocean's surface toward the ship's starboard bow.

Dr. E's warning came over the comms: "Small rubber raft on the stern. Launch micro-drones."

Luna and James released miniature drones, cameras whirring as they darted in. "Roger," Luna confirmed, eyes glued to the feed.

## The Vessel Insertion

Zane and Austin walked across the iceberg for a clean HRAM leap, switched to RGM, and vaulted to the side of the ship like it was nothing. Sticky, adaptive soles and gloves clinging to the iced-over hull, moving in perfect sync. They scaled the side and sent micro-crawlers through the cabin windows. Live video revealed two shadows whispering.

Hardee's alert lit their HUDs: "Desmond is on a call."

## The Conspiracy Unfolds

"Desmond, we've almost got the whale, but it's tangled. RIPTIDE's top hunters are on it. Hurry, it will fund Slate's campaign. TIDES funding should be ours. Corbin's intel timed the fake broadcast to pull Hardee away. Move before this blows."

Silence. Every piece snapped into place: illegal poaching, political conspiracy, the Vales' betrayal.

## Underwater

Puck and Tad slipped beneath the glassy sea. Their suits hummed warmth, sonar tracers glowing bioluminescent in the deep blue. Ghostly ice shards drifted around them as they located a great whale, its bulk tangled in netting attached to cables. Tad's plasma blade carved through cables; Puck's directional sonic pulse loosened the mesh. With a final, powerful thrust, the whale shot upward in a triumphant breach, sending a towering spray of icy water into the air.

## Surface Action

Puck and Tad surfaced together, firing TENDRIL grapples to the deck, hoisting themselves upward towards the deck. They landed in perfect sync, knees bent, arms level, a display of timeless strength and unity.

Luna and James turned the corner around the bow of the ship. Their drones mapped the angles for approach to the rubber raft and uploaded the data to their HUDs. Luna launched a TENDRIL to bind a RIPTIDE agent. James followed, ensnaring another in sticky bio-goo.

## The Deck Takedown

Within the cabin, Zane and Austin deployed ink-cloud projectors from their arm mounts. A swirling, harmless mist enveloped the room; startled crewmen fumbled taser sticks, accidentally striking one another and collapsing in surprise. "Easy pickings," Zane whispered, trying not to laugh. "Let's employ TENDRIL restraints and check their vitals," Austin grinned. Zane and Austin released their TENDRIL cuffs and secured both subjects. Their nano-infused bio gear projected the scan to their HUDs. "Healthy as ever. Maybe some mental concerns, but not related to clocking each other on the noggin," Austin quibbled.

51

## The Final Preparations

With the poachers contained and the whale free, Puck's voice rang out over comms, calm and unwavering: "Justice and mercy both served. We've recorded every moment. It's time to go public."

Seconds later, Dr. E's voice chimed in from the Forge Halo Hub. "Coast Guard inbound under IWC and Canadian–Greenland treaties, ETA three by helo...so choppa-choppa, team. Prep for hand-off. Derrick, Jones, and Jonah are encoding video and audio from the comms tower, getting ready for the presentation. Excellent work, team."

Puck inhaled the crystalline Arctic air, resolve shining across his visor, a smirk beneath his facemask that you could almost see. The Coast Guard helicopter appeared on the horizon, ready to assert federal jurisdiction. This was no ordinary environmental victory; it was spiritual warfare waged with truth, unity, and faith.
"Team," he said into comms, voice steady, "the shadows have been unveiled."

## Senate Oversight Hearing

Back in the chamber, Senator Emory Slate paced before the lectern, brow creased, as he addressed the room, "The Shell Tech Corporation is a professional company making advancements in environmental research for the advancement of humanity. They were conducting important research before these thugs interfered and disrupted a legitimate operation.
This so-called Team TIDES operates in secret, leaps to conclusions, and wastes taxpayer dollars on stunts instead of real progress. Something must be done."

The Speaker rapped the gavel. "Agent Hardee, your response?"

Hardee rose, measured but resolute. "When you funded Team TIDES, you entrusted us with a mission handed down from forefathers: Teamwork, Integrity, Dedication, Excellence, Service. Today, we deliver on that promise."

He lifted his gauntlet. "Our technology is neither a hero nor a villain. A knife can kill or free a captive; its purpose is defined by the hand that wields it. We choose to serve others, protect creation, and uphold justice."

He nodded once. "The evidence you requested is here. View our footage from the last 24 hours, then judge. Meet the team, Team TIDES Align!"

## A Show of Truth

At Hardee's command, every member activated Echo-Sync HRAM Mode. In perfect unison, they vaulted skyward, thrusters blazing towards the hearing room. Hardee tapped his arm gauntlet, and nanobots constructed a drone with HD video projection. "You're about to witness the unveiling of shadows. Our Show of Truth begins now."

Screens behind him ignited in a cascade of video footage: laughter and urgent strategy huddles in the Vaultrium; crimson-tinted currents of RIPTIDE's toxic runoff snaking through once-pristine shores; the full environmental output readings with evidence of the redtide, the fierce duel with Eclipse's corrosive goo and Ironshade's pulse-shattering forceful strikes; Sinclair's deliverance and rebirth as Jonah Freeman; and the Arctic siege transmission, the freed whale, poachers unmasked, and the Vale cousins caught in their own broadcast. Even Slate's eye twitched at the sight of his operatives laid bare, a momentary flicker of dread before fury contorted his features.

He sprang to his feet, thrusting the contents of the desk airborne. One clipboard was hurled toward a bystander. Hardee's TENDRIL lashed out in a single, fluid arc, snatching the clipboard mid-air and dropping it harmlessly at his feet. Scarlet with rage, Senator Slate lunged toward the exit but was intercepted by two stone-faced security officers.

"What sorcery is this?" he thundered. "I will not stand for this theater!"

The Speaker slammed the gavel. "Order! Security, stand ready."

Hardee inclined his head toward the guard. "Thank you."

A hush fell across the chamber. All eyes locked on Hardee's composed stance as he stepped forward, voice firm but calm. "This," he said, holding up the gauntlet, "is TENDRIL, a product of partnership, research, and sound science. Tools like this don't come with morality; only the hand that wields them decides their purpose. A hammer builds or destroys. A lens exposes or blinds. It's not the tech, it's the truth behind its use."

He scanned the room, then added, "You've all seen the same events, yet some have arrived at wildly different conclusions.

That's what happens when you operate in shadows. Truth doesn't hide. It reveals. It aligns. And only the light can expose what deception conceals." He tapped his comm once more. This time with resolve in his voice. "TIDES, randezvous on the veranda."

A more precise command for everyone to step out into the light of day to display the Truth and meet the team that worships the living God.

The words echoed through the chamber like a call to arms. The light emerged as the 3D holographic feed from Hardee's drone flared to life. "Everyone," he said, voice resonating through the hall, "meet Team TIDES as they are en route."

The hologram displayed live feeds of each team member glowing in sequence.

Streamed from their in-flight HUDs, the team connected to their audience as they approached the hearing. The team was staggered but in coordinated formation, responding to the call from every corner of their respective missions. Some had already arrived and waited just beyond the doors. Others were in mid-air, converging like streaks of light over the skyline.

## The Team

Each member was introduced with a flash of telemetry, mission highlights, and their spoken testimonies broadcast directly to the room. One by one, they shared why they had committed to the mission: to defend the voiceless, restore what had been stolen, and stand in the gap where others had failed to show up.

The chamber shifted with tension and awe. Some in the gallery rose in applause, others squirmed in their seats or quietly slipped out, uneasy in the presence of clarity.

Hardee's gaze lingered on an empty chair, once held by Slate's aide, Desmond Vale. Vacant. Gone.

Meanwhile, at the comms tower, "Jonah, get to the transport tube. Forge briefing awaits." Jones gave him a nod. "You've already made waves; it's time to learn the currents." Jonah said, "Where you send me, I will go." Jonah stepped inside. With a whoosh, he disappeared down the transport tube, bound for briefing, training, and deeper revelations.

Back in the hearing chamber, Hardee turned back to the panel. "The facts have been shown. The light has been directed to the shadows. The only question now is, will we all continue in Truth, or retreat into shadows?"

# The Frequency of War

With the alignment completed, Hardee stepped forward, his voice firm yet inviting.

"If you'll walk with me, step outside. Come meet the team." Some continued their retreat deeper into the building, unwilling to step into the light. But others filtered into the courtyard. Outside, the team fanned out, suits glinting in the afternoon sun. People gathered around, wide-eyed at the high-tech gear, responsive armor, and personalized constructs. Tad and Puck scaled a nearby facade in Rainforest Gripper Mode, bounding between ledges like amphibious commandos.

"RGM is way easier than saying 'Rainforest Gripper Mode' every time," Puck laughed.

Tad grinned. "Yeah, but you just said it anyway."

"Don't start quoting Dr. E," Jones called out. "She's got acronyms for her acronyms." Dr. E cleared her throat over comms, "You know I can hear you two, right?" They all shared a laugh as they were settling into their feeling of victory for the day.

Families walking by gathered to see what the action was all about. Kids mimicked hoverboard stances as Austin gave a mini demo. Derrick scanned soil samples with his gauntlet, sparking a chat about local geology. Jones handed out forged metal coins engraved with the octopus moon, a symbol of their mission and mystery. Families took photos. Teens asked how to join. Older veterans nodded quietly; their respect was evident. It was a moment of connection. Of unity. Of belonging. The kind of peace Team TIDES was built to protect. Hardee made one final statement, "This team gives the credit and the glory to God, not to seek fame or reward for themselves, but for God's Truth to expose the works of darkness!" Then- The squeal of tires snapped the peace in half. A black militarized-looking vehicle skidded to a stop outside the park gate, smoke hissing from its undercarriage. The enormous rear doors slammed open.

Puck tapped his gauntlet, issuing the command, "Drone scan. Plate lock." A mini-drone launched skyward, locking onto the license plate.

"Confirmed," Jones called out. "Shell Tech Corp. It's RIPTIDE. Let's give them some credit, they registered their boat and this monster tank."

Then the earth cracked. A shockwave tore through the plaza; a distant statue toppled in a thunderous crash. Laughter died. Conversations froze.

Before the drone could finish its scan, blue and blood-orange shockwaves arced across the sidewalk, ripping up tiles and obliterating a marble bench. From the settling dust, a towering figure emerged with armor pulsing with crude technology, forearms coiled in energy projection devices that ripped objects into his field. Dr. E crackled over comms, "Seismic reading logged, blasted the Richter scale. Locking satellite scan."

The figure ripped an iron fence from the ground with the tech on his arms, bent it like it was nothing, then stomped through the plaza, lifting earth and stone, then folding a bronze eagle in half.

"Who is that?" someone whispered.

"Not here to talk," Puck replied, narrowing his gaze.

"This park's about to become a war zone," Zane warned. "Civilians everywhere."

"Scan complete," Dr. E added. "Uploading 3D threat profile to your HUDs. Magneto-Acoustic Resonance Devices and geophysics tech, now weaponized. He warps gravity and magnetism. Code name: Shatterborne. Watch your six."

Hardee stepped forward, voice firm: "Clear the square. Shield the gallery. Derrick, Brox, and Ryan...evac detail. Puck, Jones, Tad, James, flank, and analyze. Luna, Zane...sky perimeter. Watch for secondary threats. Go!"

Puck's voice cut through the team comms with sharp resolve: "TIDES-Echo Sync. Let's move!" The team burst into action, armor glinting and constructs forming in unison. Nearby, a bystander tripped over a loose stone. Derrick caught him mid-fall, leaped over a stone wall, and put him down safely. Tad directed sonic blasts at airborne concrete, thrown at civilians, turning it to dust and pebbles. Luna hovered above in Flight Mode before shifting into RGM atop a nearby ledge, her grips anchoring her as she scanned rooftops for backup threats. Zane streaked across the plaza, running short-grid searches in Flight Mode for hidden assailants. As Puck's visor locked on Shatterborne across the square. The TIDES HUD flashed "Primary Threat," and a deep certainty stirred in his chest. They weren't invincible. They were humans, nearly spent from an already relentless day. This wasn't just a battle; it was a signal. They'd struck a nerve. Team TIDES was rising, and their enemies knew it. If they couldn't win by wits, then force. Puck, Tad, Jones, and James converged on Shatterborne with incredible speed. He was ready. With a twist of his forearms, the coils on his arms thrummed to life. He unleashed a concussive blast at a marble statue of a soldier, sending it toppling. A nearby couple, a man and his wife, froze as if time stood still. Puck rocketed a TENDRIL toward them, but in the swirl of dust and stone, it missed its mark by inches. The TENDRIL snagged only the tail of the man's open jacket, yanking him sideways as the statue crashed down. Stone splintered against bone, a sickening crack, as the colossal figure landed atop the man's arm, pinning him to the ground. Puck roared in frustration but didn't hesitate. He whipped out a secondary goo net that erupted around Shatterborne, sticky filaments weaving across the villain's chest and arms. Before Shatterborne could tear it off, Puck slammed a focused sonic pulse into the mesh, staggering him backward into a broken fountain. That brief opening was all Tad and Jones needed.

Together, they surged forward in HRAM, muscles bulging through the nanofiber weave, and hoisted the statue free, lifting it clear of the pinned man. With the debris moved, Jones scooped him into a medical pod construct as Tad formed a goo patch on the man's forearm that doubled as a vitals monitor. The HUD read a broken forearm with bleeding, but otherwise stable. The visor immediately dispatched multiple emergency rescue teams.

The wife's scream cut through the chaos: "Look what you've done to my husband! You had to confront these thugs! If you'd let them be, none of this would've happened!" Puck's visor reflected her tears, but there was no time to console her. Derrick and James formed another medical pod, and the team lifted the couple away from danger, spiraling up and out of the plaza. Moments later, they set them down gently at a secure clearing where TIDES EMS could render further aid. Shatterborne was breaking free of his netting, and Luna cried out over coms, "Tad, what's that? There's a tree turning brown like it's dying rapidly about a block behind you to your left!" Tad spun in mid-air, visor pinging the garden. "Attempting target lock... fast, agile signature. Coordinates sent to the Vaultrium for a deeper scan. Dr. E, are you reading this?" "Trying echo-ping now," Dr. E's voice crackled. "Hold... he's too mobile."

Tad darted closer, weaving between benches and hedges. Suddenly, the dark-suited figure halted, raised both forearms, and a low hum built to a roar, vines and leaves ripped free as a localized vortex sucked in the surrounding flora. Tad seized the moment, locking coordinates and transmitting to Dr. E: "Locked on. Scan and identify!"

A heartbeat later, Dr. E replied, "Got it. He's equipped with a bio-reactor pack that ingests organic material via dual suction lines on his forearms. Onboard nanoprocessors molecularly

decompose plant matter and reforge it into toxic sludge, acid fog, or mutagenic ooze. He's weaponizing the environment itself, essentially a portable decomposition-recomposition lab. He uses the surrounding greenery as his ammunition. Full profile uploading to your HUD-caution: his output can corrode protective armor and disrupt our situational control. Code-named: Terrablight."

The feed blinked live into each visor, rendering Terrablight's silhouette as pulsing biobreath coils and glowing suction hoses. As Puck's jaw clenched, the clear scientific threat filled the comms: nature perverted into weaponry, and Team TIDES would have to adapt quickly. The team was feeling exhausted. They were facing not one but two serious threats. Even as that registered, Shatterborne tore free of Puck's net and let out a deafening roar. He aimed his gauntlets, reversing the pulsed fields, and in an instant, the earth beneath a trio of terrified bystanders buckled. Metal grates yanked upward, rocks levitated, and the three were torn from their feet.

"Group of three, edge of the plaza near town!" Zane shouted, diving in Flight Mode, but the disrupted grav-fields buffeted his suit. He overshot them, suit auto-correcting for reentry. On his second pass, Shatterborne unleashed another pulse. Zane braced, then found his balance just as the trio began falling after the field shifted. He snatched two of them in mid-plummet and constructed medical cots to carry them to safety. But the third, a young woman, was out of his reach. Thankfully, the disrupted gravity field gave Puck enough time to react.

"Puck!" Zane's voice cracked in comms. Puck cut across the plaza on his hoverboard, momentum slicing through chaos. He fired dual sticky-goo nets upward, weaving a living hammock that arrested her fall. She slipped unconscious into its embrace. Puck caught her gently, scanning her vitals through the mesh. HUD vitals reading "Fainting, monitor for recovery."

He scooped her into a sealed medical construct as Zane and the others rallied. "Transport site, now!" Puck barked. Within moments, they delivered all three to the TIDES EMS staging area. They were shaken, with minor injuries, but alive. Shatterborne and Terrablight regrouped, earth and flora still quaking, their enemies' devastating duo forging ahead. Derrick and Hardee worked side-by-side, herding civilians behind the shelter behind a building. The local PD slung tape across the street, their hands raised in steady lines to keep onlookers at bay. From the edge of the flowerbeds, Terrablight's bio-reactor whirred, spitting out a sizzling jet of mutagenic ooze that ate through the terrain.

"Cover his bio-sludge with our counteragent," Dr. E's voice crackled in every HUD. "It'll slow the reaction, but you're fighting a flood."

Luna dove low in Flight Mode, then snapped into Rainforest Gripper Mode on the garden's highest trellis. "Toxic runoff's spreading fast! We need to cut off his supply." She fired two micro-drones that clamped onto the hoses snaking from his backpack, pinching them before they could siphon more plant matter, but Terrablight was able to rip them free in a few moments.

Meanwhile, Zane and Ryan flanked Shatterborne's position. Zane fired a TENDRIL that formed a tripwire behind Shatterborne's legs. At the same moment, Ryan vaulted in HRAM. His TENDRIL snatched and slung a piece of broken statue that was airborne beside Shatterborne, slamming it into the villain's midsection and sending him reeling as his legs caught on the tripwire.

Puck and James pressed the advantage. Puck lobbed focused sticky-goo nets that wrapped one forearm coil; James' echoing TENDRIL ensnared the other, yanking it taut around a sturdy oak. Breathing hard, Puck aimed a sonic pulse at the brute, shocking Shatterborne's exosuit in a glittering wave of energy that rippled across his armor. The suit mechanics flickered. Terrablight whirled, backpack glowing sickly green. He unleashed a rolling acid fog that corroded the plaza's stonework, blistering Puck's armor. Tad slammed into him from above with a sonic blast strike that knocked Terrablight down, but the ground beneath them was buckling, fissures cracking toward the crowd.

Hardee swooped in, scooping up the nearest bystanders and vaulting them to safety atop nearby rooftops. "Everyone clear!" he exclaimed, then locked eyes with Luna. "Chopper inbound!"

Over the roar of engines, an extraction helicopter descended with a large metal platform. Through the swirling dust, the Vale cousins, Desmond and Corbin, stood in the open side door of the massive chopper, smirking as they signaled the crew. In moments, both villains were hoisted from the battleground. As the chopper lifted off, its silhouette backlit by the setting sun, the Vales waved mockingly to Team TIDES with smiles of triumph etched on their faces.

Down below, the team watched them go, armor scorched, gear damaged, and hearts heavy with the sting of a narrow miss.

They could've chased. They could've tried harder. But they were spent. Their mission today was no longer about winning. They had people to protect.

"We didn't win this battle, did we?" Puck said softly, voice weighted by resolve and weariness.

Luna placed a gloved hand on his shoulder, quiet, steady. Neither of them spoke further.

As the thrum of the chopper faded into the darkening sky, the team gathered. Bruised. Burnt. Silenced. They began strolling through the remnants of the plaza, boots crunching...

...across shattered stone and scorched grass. They weren't scanning for enemies anymore. They were looking for the forgotten. The ones still hurting.

And then they saw it-the statue.

Once, it had stood tall: a marble soldier, standing firm, eyes set on the horizon. Now, it lay in ruin. One arm was shattered. Its shield was broken. The blood was fresh, real, human blood still marked the cracked base where it had crushed the man they had pulled free.

The team paused. Nobody spoke at first.

Puck finally broke the silence. "That statue stood for sacrifice. For what we're supposed to be."

Tad shook his head, jaw tight. "Now it's just... broken."

"It's broken," Puck echoed quietly. "Like we feel. That man's hurt. And so are we."

No one disagreed.

They stood there, silent, staring at the fallen monument. What once stood for valor now mirrored their failure. The weight of every loss, every cry for help they didn't reach in time, pressed down like gravity.

Jones looked away. "We were supposed to make it better."

"We will," Luna said, her voice low, raw. "But not today."

Derrick turned as local EMS and fire crews arrived. Some approached cautiously, others with quiet nods of respect. Then a retired firefighter stepped forward, soot-streaked, silver-haired, with worn hands and deep lines around his eyes. He held out a bottle of water.

"You did what you could," he said, voice like gravel and smoke. "And more than most ever do."

Hardee stepped forward to meet him. "Didn't feel like enough."

"It never does," the fireman said simply. "But you stood between destruction and the people. That matters."

Luna's voice cracked. "But people still got hurt."

He nodded. "People always get hurt. But that doesn't mean we stop showing up."

He looked at the statue, then at each of them, bruised, weary, and hearts bowed under the weight of it all.

"People say if God were real, He wouldn't let this kind of pain happen. But they don't realize there's evil in this world because there's free will. God never made puppets. Not men. Not angels. We all get to choose. That's where evil comes from, not Him."

He paused, letting the words breathe.

"You want to know what I've learned in twenty-six years of public service? It's faith. I've seen miracles come from rubble, and hope pulled from ashes. The stories you'll hear from survivors, the ones who trust God even after tragedy, those are the ones that change you. Evil doesn't win just because it shows up. It only wins if people stop showing up to answer the call. Evil is defeated already...just answer the call on your life and do your part."

The team stood still, taking it in. The man gestured toward the statue. "That marble soldier? He's cracked, yeah. But he isn't destroyed. That blood on the stone? That's not failure. That's the price of trying and laying yourself down. Blood pays the price. Life is in the blood."

He glanced at each of them. "You're hurting. But your hurt means your heart's still working. That matters. Get up, show up, and do it again tomorrow. And again after that. Pick up the cross every day."

A few civilians slowly approached. They were bandaged, bruised, and limping. No cheering. No applause. Just a quiet presence. One woman touched Tad's arm gently, eyes glassy.

"Thank you," she whispered.

The words hit harder than any villain's weapon.

It didn't fix everything. But it was something.

The sky had surrendered to dusk, and the storm of battle faded into distant sirens and the receding hum of service vehicles. For Team TIDES, the real fight had just begun, inside themselves. They were bone-tired, hollow from every life they'd tried to save. Their armor, once luminous, bore scorch marks and cracked plating, proof that their nanobots hadn't had time to mend. Echo Sync flickered in and out, their connection as frayed as their spirits.

Every face they passed stared at them with a mix of awe and fear, which was a reminder that they still had people to protect, even when they felt they had nothing left in the tank.

They needed to heal.

Puck rose and held out his battered gauntlet. "Team, watches down. Plain clothes." In unison, their suits receded, nanobots retracting into their Tide Bands. Echo Sync went dark. "We're people right now, frightened, flawed," he said, voice shaking. "Let's pray."

They formed a loose circle, grabbed hands, and bowed their heads.

"Father, we feel that we have failed to stop this tonight. Take us from feeling to faith, placing our hope and trust in your hands. Guide us and give us strength to rise again, for every life, every scar, every soul. Bless the injured and the broken, heal their wounds. Father, we bless our enemies to see the light, answer to Truth, and turn from evil and back to you like Jonah, and all of us have. Give us what we need to carry on. Make us strong again so we can bless others. Let us learn from this. We bless your holy name. In Jesus' name we pray and agree."

72

"Amen" echoed around him, raw and real. Hardee stepped forward, resting a hand on Puck's shoulder. "Thank you. We needed that."

Still wordless, they trudged to a late-night diner whose neon sign buzzed like a heartbeat. Coffee orders came, black or with cream, and soon the table was littered with half-eaten bacon, pancakes, and steaming mugs.

James stirred his cream into his coffee, watching it swirl. "Does the cream get darker... or the coffee whiter?"

Jordan blinked. "You know we can't solve existential crises in a mug, right?"

Tad grinned. "Still worth a shot."

They laughed softly at first, then louder, tears soaking napkins as the ache in their chests eased by a fraction.

Breaking has its purpose: new cracks let grace shine in.

A crusty, gray-muzzled police captain in turnout gear stepped around the corner, hat under his arm. "I'm Captain Williams, North Precinct. Saw the feed and you all out there. Why do bad things happen to people? I've heard that before. I've fought crime for thirty years, pulled people from wrecks, and watched strangers pray me through my darkest nights. Evil is real, but so is grace. The fact that we can see the difference between right and wrong shows us who we are. You showed up when others ran away. That matters. We don't need to be perfect to make a difference. Nobody's perfect. Except one."

He paused, eyes softening. "When you're at your lowest, remember the lives you helped. Healing starts when someone shows up. Then you rise again, like resurgents."

Puck looked at Captain Williams, "Thank you, you're another God-send. Another voice of confirmation and edification."

Then, Puck caught Hardee's eye. "I have to see the man from the statue." Hardee nodded. "We'll go now." They all thanked Captain Williams and left money on the table, stepping into the cool night.

Puck tapped his Tide Band. Echo Sync flared back to life, stronger now, reforged by their shared fragility. He hailed the Vaultrium.

"Dr. E? The man with the broken arm, where did you take him?"

"His name is RaJohn, his wife is Shonté ," Dr. E replied. "We brought him and his wife to TIDES Hospital. Dr. Christenson's already patched him up using our latest nano-cast and bio-resonance therapy. Healing's underway."

Puck turned to the team. "Who's with me?"

"I am," James said without hesitation.

"We're in," Brox and Ryan answered together.

"We all are," Luna added, her voice steady.

Their suits reformed, nanobots weaving armor back together into Flight Mode.

Visors locked in place and linked to the Vaultrium flight navigation system. In perfect sync, they launched into the night sky. The glow of the city below blended with the stars above. Moments later, they touched down on the hospital's rooftop.

Waiting by the helipad, Dr. Christenson greeted them. "Thank you for coming. RaJohn's stable and very chatty. His wife hasn't left his side."

They followed him down the quiet corridor and into a bright recovery bay. RaJohn stood beside a bio-bed, his arm encased in a high-tech nano-cast. Shonté smiled at the sight of the team.

"This goo tingles, but it works fast," RaJohn said, grinning.

"Mind if I show you something?" "Lead the way," Puck nodded. As they walked, RaJohn spoke with purpose. "I've been where you are. That weight on your chest, it's real. I served in combat zones. And today? Those attackers weren't trying to take you out directly. They went after soft targets.

Civilians. Emotional anchors. That wasn't weakness; it was strategy. And you countered it the only way real heroes do: you put yourselves last."

They reached a wide recovery room filled with about fifteen people, civilians rescued from the plaza, being checked and bandaged by TIDES med-techs. Some were laughing softly, others resting. One familiar face turned as they entered.

"Wes?" Puck asked.

"The one and only," Wes grinned. "Things got hectic fast, but your team moved like clockwork. I work for Senator Johnson now; he's a big backer of the Team TIDES initiative. When I heard what happened, I came to help."

He gestured around the room. "Take a walk. These folks want to thank you. And Puck, thanks again for including me back during that river cleanup. It meant more than you know."

A young woman in a sling stepped forward. "I was falling when the rubble hit. I don't even know who caught me. But I'm walking because of you."

An older man with a stitched coat added, "My grandson was nearly buried under falling debris; your shielding saved us both."

Others echoed in:

"I couldn't breathe in that fog. You pulled me out in time."

"You got us to safety, seconds before the collapse."

The gratitude poured out like a healing balm.

RaJohn, watching closely, spoke softly. "You see it now? This is why you fight. Every life you touch, every moment you choose grace over giving up, it matters." Hardee placed a hand on Puck's shoulder. "We did more than we thought." RaJohn nodded. "Evil will always rise, but so will grace. Rise with it. And if you ever need another hand... I'm ready." His wife stepped up beside him, placing a hand gently on Puck's arm. "I owe you all an apology. I lashed out from fear.

76

He's always rushed toward danger, and it's hard not to try to hold him back. But this, what you're doing, is right. You don't bear the blame for the evil in the world. You're standing in front of it. Prepared. Purposeful. Just like he's always tried to do."

Puck smiled gently. "Thank you. That means more than you know."As they turned to head back toward the helipad, RaJohn and his wife walked with them. Their armor, though polished and whole, still held the imprint of the night. But in their hearts, something had shifted.

They had been broken, but not beaten. Scarred, but not scattered. They had risen, not just as warriors, but as protectors. Spread out across the rooftop helipad and hailed the rest of the team at base. Puck turned to RaJohn, "Thank you for showing us. We will see you soon. Rest that arm and listen to Dr. Christenson. Have a good evening." Nanobots sealed up their helmets. Puck hailed command, "Vaultrium, we're coming home!" "Doors wide open," Dr. E chimed in. "Sky's all clear, fly fast!" Dr. Zayler finished. They'd faced the worst of the night and found grace in the ashes.

As they lifted off, the city lights fell away beneath them. In the quiet hum of their suits, sorrow turned to laughter, memories of small victories, shared jokes, and the knowledge that they'd saved lives, even when they felt they'd failed. This was what it meant to overcome: to get back up, again and again. To rise with the tides. To be guardians, built not by perfection, but by persistence, one heart-setback at a time.

They eased into formation, heading back to the Forge's Vaultrium. Home. A place of rest, of healing, of fellowship. Tonight, it was time to unwind. Because in this marathon of mission and mercy, every scar was a lesson and every lesson a step closer to reaching the finish line.

The hour of night was growing late, but finally they were home. They touched down in the Forge's Vaultrium. The soft, steady hum of the chamber brought a measure of peace to their frayed nerves. Their teammates, Jonah, Dr. E, Dr. Zayler, Celeste, and others, gathered around, relief shining in their eyes.

Dr. E stepped forward. "Suit systems check and deep-clean. We'll patch up your Tide Bands," she said, collecting their watches and handing each a fresh band, just in case duty called again. As their spirits needed repair, so did their armor. They'd earned this moment of restoration. James helped place the bands into the nano-restoration chamber, which sprang to life with a gentle pulse. Hardee's voice cut through the hum. "Team, physical first. Showers, and reach out to loved ones; they've been waiting for good news. Then, and only then, meet me in the common room. We'll debrief, share lessons, and plan our next move. Every voice matters."

Puck paused in the hallway, his hand on the cool metal panel. A diagram formed in his mind: Lift up → Flow down → Serve out → Pour out again. Service and love radiate from each of them. First upward toward God, then down from Him, cascading back through the team, and finally outward. That was true leadership: the servant's heart. He thought of the cycle of water that gives life to every corner of creation and Christ's words, "I am the living water." A deeper meaning stirred, a reminder that we are the vessels, jars of clay, and He lives in us. A small spark of renewal lit his spirit as he continued down the hall to freshen up.

They split off down echoing corridors. In private quarters, each tapped a comm-link, calling family and loved ones. Voices shifted from relief to laughter as they recounted small victories. These connections, heart to heart, were as vital as any repair protocol.

78

Soon they gathered in the Vaultrium common room. Hardee nodded to the team. "Floor is yours."

Luna: "I learned to watch my angles, never assume the skyline is safe."

James: "Our constructs adapted in real time, but we need more tools and design input."

Brox: "Strength without precision risks collateral, sharpened focus on the next round."

Ryan: "Medical-evac protocols worked... but I want a secondary fail-safe: mass shielding."

Puck: "After mass shielding for soft targets... precise insertion like a scalpel to disease."

Dr. E and Dr. Zayler took notes and looked at the team when they were all done, "We have got this covered. We will get on it and then some. We have some things cooking already."

At the end, heads bowed.

Puck's voice was quiet but firm:

"Father, we're broken but not beaten. Thank you for hearing us tonight. Grant us the courage to rise again. Amen."

A chorus of "Amen" lifted the weight in the room.

They laughed, softly at first, then more freely, as Hardee quipped, "That coffee was good with cream." Tears and smiles mingled. They were a team again, battle-scarred but bonded. Puck cleared his throat. "Tomorrow: Jonah's first Synchronium session, and I want RaJohn and Shonté here for strategy and spirit. Who's in?"

A ripple of nods:
"I am."
"We're in."
"We all are."

Dr. Zayler pulled the specks up on a holographic table. "Dr. Christenson cleared RaJohn for light duty until noon. He'll trial that prototype biomechanical shielding we designed. First field test."

Austin grinned. "Government ops meet high-tech heroics, love it! I've uploaded Shatterborne and Terrablight toxin profiles to the server. Analytics by morning."

Dr. E tapped her comm. "Perfect. We'll review Eclipse and Ironshade scans in training. Adaptation can't wait. Nothing would survive the fallout otherwise. Calculated precision isn't by chance."

As the clock struck midnight, Hardee raised his hand.

"Rest up. Tomorrow has enough in store. Jonah, Matt's quarters are yours, or take a guest suite. This droid can guide you. Good night, team."

They dispersed into the hush of their private quarters. Puck crawled into his bed by the porthole, moonlight shimmering through the water outside the window. His Tide Band glowed softly, a beacon of light in the darkness, unity in the body working together, and the promise of a new dawn. Tonight, their bodies would repair and heal as they rested.

He tapped his comm. "Tad, you there?" "I was just about to call you," Tad answered. "This is incredible... isn't it? Hard, but mixed with rewards for following our call. It all started with talking about frogmen in Starlight Cove."

"Yeah," Puck agreed, leaning back into the shine of moonlight by the porthole. "Nobody said this would be easy, but it's worth every moment. We never know what each day will bring. That's why we stay ready. You doing okay?"

Tad's voice was steady: "It's a lot to take in, but I can't imagine walking away. This is a lifelong commitment. How about you?"

Puck stretched and settled in. "Wouldn't miss it for the world. Sleep well, brother. Just wanted to check in. Good night."

They signed off, and the lights faded.

80

# Turn of the Tides

The next morning, the team gathered in the common room beside the kitchen, the scent of coffee and sizzling bacon weaving through the air. It felt like a rare moment of peace, a soft landing after a storm.

Puck and James manned the coffee station, trading jabs over whose brew was stronger. Jones, Jonah, Brox, and Ryan handled the stove, flipping eggs and crisping bacon with the confidence of a seasoned diner crew. Pajama pants, slippers, and bedhead ruled the room: no dramatic entries, no glowing constructs, just teammates relaxing in the comfort of shared space.

Zane set the table with quiet intention, while Jordan, Derrick, Luna, and Tad pitched in, filling cups, grabbing napkins, and pulling chairs into place. It was casual. Unhurried. Something they hadn't realized they needed until they were living in it.

Dr. E, Agent Hardee, Dr. Zayler, and Celeste entered last, pausing in the doorway with faint smiles. The sight was refreshing, after a night that nearly broke them, this was healing: joy in simplicity, laughter in rest, strength rediscovered in unity.

They had walked through fire the day before, pruned, challenged, and humbled. But like a tree trimmed back, new buds of growth were already visible in their words, their bonds, their renewed sense of purpose.

They lingered for hours, refilling plates, sharing quiet stories, simply being present.

Eventually, the room quieted. Puck leaned back and slapped his thigh with a grin. "Who's ready for action?"

Dr. E stood, eyes twinkling. "We've got the green light from Dr. Christenson. RaJohn and Shonté are clear for pickup." She raised a brow. "How about bringing them in style? Octopod tunnel transport?"

Tad and Zane nearly jumped from their seats.

"Yes!" Tad grinned. "Some of you haven't been in one yet, you don't know what you're missing!"

"Fifteen minutes," Puck called out. "Meet at the tunnel access in the Vaultrium!"

The team scattered. Dishes clinked. Tide Bands activated. Echo Sync flickered to life as suits emerged in a swarm of nanobots, wrapping around them with precision. Some selected Frogman Mode; others suited up for cockpit piloting octopods engineered for rapid deployment, tight maneuverability, and adaptive navigation in any environment. On the way to Frogman Bay, the team piloting Octos remotely selected and started their chosen pod.

By the time they reached the tunnel platform, the octopods were ready, sleek crafts lined with bioluminescent tracers, shaped like elegant creatures from the deep. Their articulated limbs and propulsion systems shifted, a quiet pulsing, as they powered up. Inside, HUDs blinked alive within translucent domes.

One by one, the team boarded or dove into formation, submerging into the crystal-blue current that led from the Forge to TIDES Hospital. The tunnel curved gently, rimmed with glowing rings that pulsed in sequence. In the tunnels and throughout the open areas of lakes connecting other tunnels, marine life flickered past schools of fish, swaying aquatic plants, and the etched remnants of a cutting machine with hydro-blade tech from the original team's handiwork. It was more than a transport. It was a return to purpose, a reminder of what they were fighting for. The beauty of creation. The mystery of the deep. A quiet undercurrent of the calling that flowed through each of them. Ahead, the octopods' lights flared against the shimmer of the hospital bay doors. In moments, they would greet RaJohn and bring him home. Beginning the next wave of preparation. Because the tides were turning, and the team was riding the flow with them.

After a quick hello and some final health clearances from Dr. Christenson, plus instructions for the biomechanical shielding for his arm, RaJohn and Shonté boarded an Octopod for the ride of a lifetime. Tad and Zane flanked their pod in Frogman Mode as they glided through the underwater tunnel, giving them a grand tour of the lake system surrounding the Forge.

They descended from the western route, past jagged rock formations and etched ruins left from a previous TIDES generation. Shonté pressed her hand to the glass, mesmerized by the ribbons of bioluminescent plankton trailing behind them, stirred gently by the clean pulse propulsion.

RaJohn grinned. "Now that's a ride."

They surfaced in Frogman Bay. Soft lights glowed along the deck, mist curling around the docking bay, lining the octopods up like silent sentinels.

"Welcome to the Vaultrium," Puck said. "This is the Forge's brainstem. Everything flows from here. Design input for R&D, offensive loadouts, equipment bays, vehicle hangars, and in a few hours: the Synchronium."

James added, "A training simulator that changes based on your design input. It adapts your strategy in real time. Nano-constructs. Holomorphing terrain. Fully immersive."

RaJohn let out a low whistle. "Knew it'd be high-tech. Didn't know it'd be all this." "You haven't even seen the planes yet," Zane smirked. Dr. E added, "And wait until you see what else I am working on that does a lot more than fly." Zane turned, "Now I am the nubbie. Whatcha working on?" Dr. E just said, "Wait and see." Tad leaned in. "Flying, diving, or hover gear, which one owns your heart?" RaJohn mock-punched both Tad and Puck. "Come on now. I'm dive-ops through and through. HALO jumps into coastal insertions, sub-launches off the grid. But we were experimenting with hybrid suits, too; flight transitions always lagged on arm-thruster recovery. Your setups here? Way beyond that."

85

Puck laughed. "That's why we cross-train. I'm team Frogman for life, though."

Dr. E presented Shonté with a welcome kit of snacks and, with a familiar glint in her eye, tossed the guys a "Choppa-Choppa" without missing stride. "Snack. Walk. Talk."

Her usual whirlwind orientation landed them at the Halo Hub, a high-res tactical projection dome. Holographic scans flickered to life, RIPTIDE agents frozen mid-strike, rotating for analysis.

"Here's what you're up against," Dr. E said.

**RIPTIDE Tech Dissection & Counterthinking**

"We captured active signatures on Shatterborne and Terrablight. We also ran forensic post-op on Eclipse and Ironshade. Both vanished after hand-off, likely lifted by shell companies or embedded corruption."

Eclipse appeared first, surrounded by rings of magnetic fluid. "He uses electromagnetic field manipulation through polarized ferrofluids. His gloves secrete a nano-aerosolized mist which, once polarized, becomes semi-solid. Think ferro-gel that binds or scorches depending on field tuning.

His chest is equipped with a pulse-based EMP, low-yield, but enough to blackout tech across one city block."

Next came Ironshade.

"He's in a surgical-grade exosuit-carbon nanoweave overlaid with myomer muscle filaments. It's hardwired into his CNS with microshock boosters, which give him surgical precision and strength. EMP shielded, acoustically dampened, immune to basic signal jamming."

Dr. E rotated to Shatterborne.

"He manipulates inertial fields. Embedded gravitic pulse generators tap into tectonic harmonics-shaped seismic waves. He uses micro-gyros and polarity reversal to rupture terrain or weaponize shockwaves."

RaJohn leaned in. "That's black-market seismic suppression hardware."

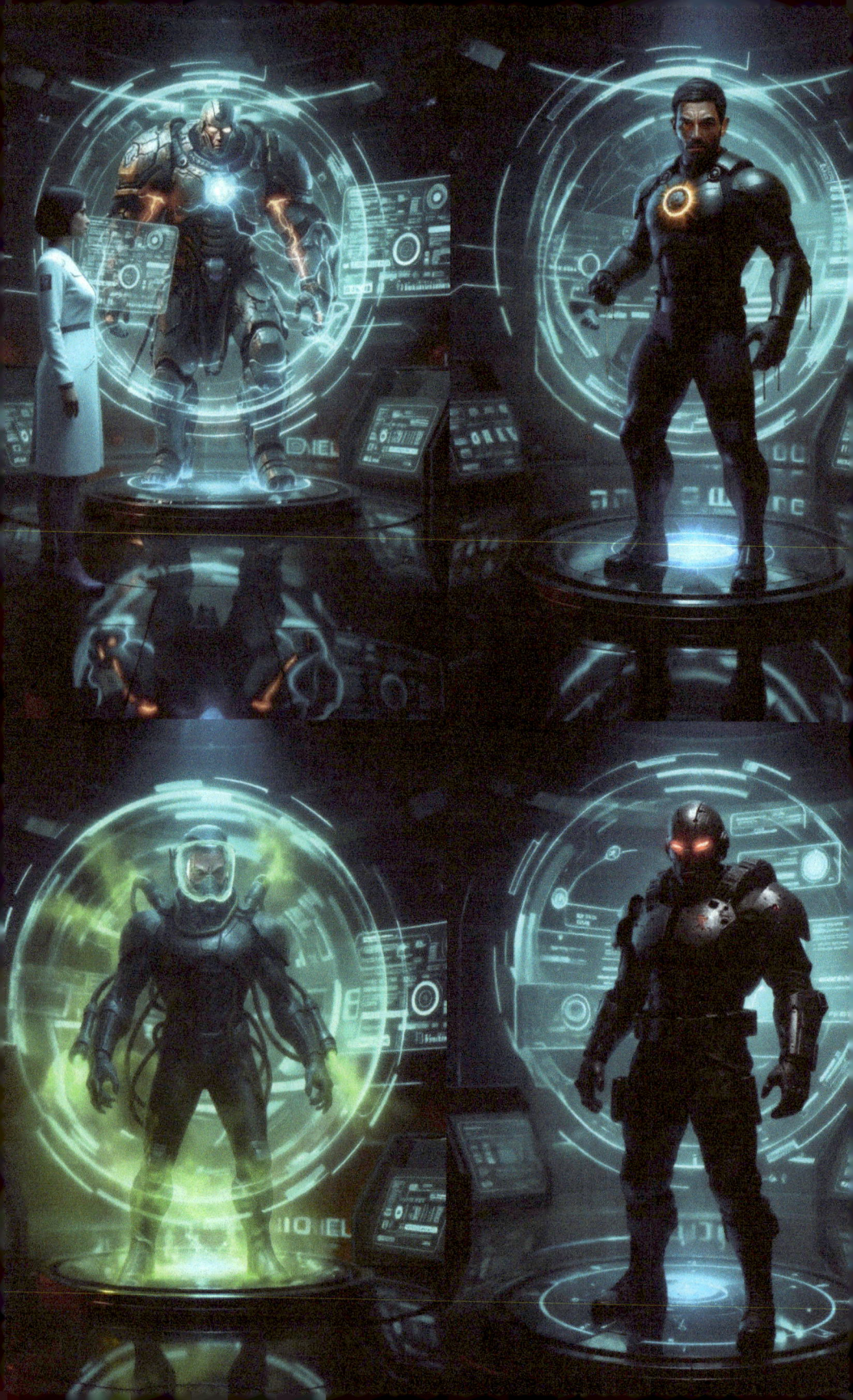

RaJohn stepped forward, his voice firm. "This is tactical corruption. Symbiosis flipped into weaponry. Someone studied eco-defense and chose to reverse it."

Dr. E nodded. "Exactly why we're fast-tracking the Symbiotic Prototype Initiative, or SPI."

Austin and Tad exchanged a grin and whispered in unison, "SPI." Dr. E caught the joke and smiled faintly before tapping her console.

From the ceiling node, a translucent schematic unfurled: double Tide Bands, belt-mounted symbiotic cubes, and a rotating archive of defensive output modes.

"These are the symbiotic cores, micro-reactive units that work in harmony with your vitals. Your breath rate, body temp, and even emotional tone are scanned and synced. The suit learns you."

She waved a hand and core modes flickered into view:

- Bio-camouflage using cephalopod chromatophores from cuttlefish, creating a shifting, mesmerizing pattern.
- Ionic detox fields to neutralize toxins like Terrablight's decay mist.
- Foam-based healing gel for rapid tissue protection.
- HRAM boost—the Hyper Reflex-Action Matrix syncing mind and reflex, plus much more.

Dr. Zayler added, "And for the first time, double Tide Bands. One for baseline control, one for layered constructs."

Dr. E leaned back, her tone steady. "And remember, SPI adapts. The cores can improvise under stress. Sometimes, it can activate features you didn't anticipate. Think of it as an auto-reflex. It may even surprise you when you need it most."

Austin tilted his head, mouthing slowly, "Cephalo... what?"

Tad snorted, "Just think, cuttlefish lights, you'll catch up."

Celeste stepped in. "If it exists in nature and has a known defense or offense system, we've studied it, coded it, and it's yours to deploy."

- Electric eel burst fields-
- Frog skin mucus shields-
- Cephalopod cloaking, dynamic camouflage, and mesmerizing-
- Bird-of-prey aerial pivoting and dive vision-

Dr. E nodded. "And there's one final piece. We call it the Heart Core."

A slow, glowing cube rotated in the center of the display. It pulsed with rhythm, like a heartbeat.

"Without it, your suit operates at standard enhanced capacity. With it? You reach near full harmonized potential."

She paused, then added, "And it carries a feature unlike anything else."

She looked around the room. "Do you remember the story of Balaam's donkey?"

Puck raised his hand. "The donkey saw what Balaam couldn't-and then God opened his mouth so he could speak."

Dr. E smiled. "Exactly. Now imagine your suit could do the same. Not by magic, but by resonance. Synced frequencies. Decoded patterns. The Heart Core taps into the language of creation itself."

Austin blinked. "You're saying... we can talk to animals?"

"Not just talk but communicate with any creature still resonating with the harmony of creation. Many animals already have language. They communicate and adapt through sonar, vibration, song, scent, or signal. In Sync Mode, your suit decodes those signals, analyzes intent, and allows two-way understanding. Your suit sends signals they can understand."

Jonah leaned forward. "A translator. For creatures."

Dr. E nodded. "Birds. Bats. Dolphins. Insects. Schools of fish. If they communicate, the suit listens and responds.

You won't control them. But you'll be able to hear their warnings... and if they trust you, they may choose to help."

Celeste added, "It's a living partnership." James pulled up visuals. "Early suit tests picked up underwater danger when fish began schooling in unnatural formations. The suit processed their stress signals before any sonar or scan detected a threat."

Dr. E turned serious. "This isn't a gimmick. It's a battlefield advantage. Birds can warn of aerial attacks. Sea life can track submerged movement. Swarms can distract, blind, or mask your escape."

Zane laughed. "Nature's got our six."

RaJohn nodded. "Organic recon. Natural defense. This changes everything."

Puck stepped closer to the schematic. "We've been fighting to protect God's creation. Now... creation fights with us."

Dr. E's voice softened. "But remember, power without balance leads to collapse. If you force it, the system shuts down. The Heart Core doesn't respond to pride. It responds to trust. It's about relationship, not control."

She stepped back. "The Heart Core is embedded in your belt band. We're syncing the final Cubes now. You'll test them soon."

Jonah closed the scan on Ironshade. "They fight with fear and brute force. We respond with balance, precision... and light."

RaJohn crossed his arms. "Eclipse and Ironshade attacked directly. Shatterborne and Terrablight target the roots, the land, the trees, the foundations. This isn't just tech, it's ideology. They're counterfeit interpreters of creation. What they corrupt... we must fight to resolve."

Puck looked to the team. "Let's talk countermeasures."

RaJohn stepped forward like a commander stepping onto a battlefield. "Modular tactics. Stay dynamic. If Shatterborne ruptures terrain, we hover. Bounce attacks.

Short-blast dampeners to break up his wave pattern," Luna added. "He's got three-minute burst cycles. That's our window."

Zane tapped his wrist-mounted schematic. "Flank him on the back swing. Drop sticky traps. Redirect the pressure."

Jonah nodded. "They love spectacle. It's their weakness. Trigger the power plays early, force them to overextend, then box them in while they're exposed."

Hardee stepped forward, quiet authority in his voice. "You're not just suiting up in tech. You're stepping into legacy. Build it right. Use it well."

RaJohn stared at the glowing Heart Core schematic, a proud smile breaking across his face.

"This is how we win. With balance. With brains. And with bonds they'll never break."

Hardee looked out over the team. "While we advance as one unit, growing tighter, smarter, and stronger, we also need to reach outward. Team TIDES cannot work in isolation. Not anymore. It's time to establish real alliances. We need trustworthy connections with local and federal agencies. If we don't build those bridges, if we don't flush out the rot hiding in our institutions, we'll be fighting spot fires for decades instead of dismantling the source."

He took a step closer to the table. "I'll be leading a secondary mission. We're going to make contact, share intelligence, and secure our network."

His eyes swept the room.

"Jordan. Derrick. Austin. Jonah. Dr. Zayler. Brox. Ryan. I need you with me, if you're willing."

There was no hesitation.

Austin grinned. "Wait, covert ops and spy work? Are you kidding? You know you're speaking my language."

Laughter rippled through the team as nods followed.

# Resonance Rising

The doors to the Synchronium hissed open, revealing a chamber pulsing with ambient light and charged energy. The floor shimmered with shifting hexagonal patterns, responding in soft waves beneath every footstep, as if the room itself acknowledged their presence. This wasn't just a training ground. It seemed alive, adaptive, and designed perfectly for their needs. An environment built to reveal more than terrain, but also a physical way to approach spiritual battles.

As the team stepped inside, the environment flickered, reading vitals, calibrating terrain, and matching familiarity to intent. This was where instincts were sharpened, where strategy became reflex. Where every construct, tactic, and movement aligned with purpose.

"Let's align," Puck said, stepping into the center of the room. "Let's find our frequency."

The team closed in, shoulder to shoulder, gearing up for their most dynamic training session yet. Ahead lay a mission to expose the works of darkness, but first, they had to sync deeper than ever before.

Dr. E entered from the side corridor, displaying two crucial upgrades: a second wristband and the belt-mounted Heart Core Module.

"Everything will make more sense once you're synced," Dr. E explained. "The interface will feel like it's thinking with you now. Fluid, and once we finish the SPIs, even more responsive."

Tad cracked a grin. "There it is. I've been waiting for this moment."

Dr. E chuckled and tossed him a Choppa-Choppa. "You know the rules. Choppa up. Time to get cracking, we've got SPI cores to finalize. We'll see you in a few hours."

The room fell quiet as all eyes turned to Jonah and RaJohn, suiting up for the first time.

Their suits flowed over them like liquid armor, adapting in record time, sealing with precision, quickly finalizing their final suit rendering to personal preferences. RaJohn's protective arm technology bonded seamlessly with the nano-suit. Then it began, Sync Mode activation.

The team dropped into fluid formations without hesitation, surrounding RaJohn and Jonah like a living net of motion and instinct. Foundational drills unfolded with clockwork coordination: fluid mode transitions, environmental adaptation, and the constantly advancing techniques of modern Team TIDES.

TENDRILs snapped into motion, flexible grappling extensions, acting like living limbs.

RGM systems launched them up walls and across terrain in seamless wall runs.

HRAM boosted their coordination into near-symbiotic precision.

They moved like water, flexible but forceful.

Puck called out, "Remember, the suit studies you, but you train each other. That's where our edge is." Their speed, strength, balance, and reaction times sharpened. Constructs formed faster. Offense and defense blurred into a single, fluid rhythm.

But it wasn't just about physicality. Something deeper was syncing.

Like the Body of Christ designed to function under one Head, they were aligning with one another, adapting in real-time, learning, responding, and supporting. It wasn't something that happened once and was finished. It had to be a consistent and repetitive act, an ongoing choice.

They weren't just fighting. They were fellowshipping.

Team TIDES wasn't built for glory. They were forged for harvest, to rescue, to guard, and to act with purpose.

As Jonah and RaJohn locked into sync like seasoned veterans, the atmosphere shifted.

James stepped forward and cued the next phase.
"Let's revisit the battle that nearly tore us apart, Shatterborne and Terrablight. It is uploaded to the Synchronium Matrix Core."
A heavy silence gripped the room.
Before symbiotic cubes.
A chance to find their resonance.
Back when the odds were stacked, and hearts were cracked.
Now they would relive it with strategy.
Hardee nodded toward RaJohn.
"Walk us through it, field-style. Show us what we missed. Because high-tech gear without intelligent planning? That's just a wasted resource."
RaJohn stepped forward slowly, his voice low but steady.
"It's not about what you carry, it's about how you move, what you observe, and how you respond under pressure. Every enemy has a rhythm. Every rhythm has a break. Our job is to find it... and strike."
The simulation lit up. The battle replayed in raw, unfiltered clarity.
"Now," RaJohn continued, gesturing to the unfolding holomap, "let's make sure we don't waste the pain we already paid for."
He moved like a veteran planning a no-fail op, where hesitation meant lives lost. He emphasized the first principle: protect civilians, then counter with speed. Never move without purpose. Watch for the enemy's tells, pre-blast patterns, posture shifts, and reaction lags.
Then he layered the real skill: multitasking in the field.
Coordinated offense.
Drone support.
Stacked non-lethal strikes in overlapping formations.
"Think wider," RaJohn instructed. "This isn't linear. Don't fixate. Engage from the air, ground, and flanks to create pressure from multiple vectors.

"If we're locked on one threat, we're blind to the one coming behind us."
Tunnel vision kills.
The words landed like a challenge and a charge.
The team absorbed it fast, synced, sharp, and adaptable.
They stopped just reacting. They began to anticipate.
They saw the field no longer as a flat surface, but as a living, breathing, 3-dimensional battlefield.
Height. Width. Depth.
Spirit. Mind. Body.
RaJohn pressed them forward. "You want the edge? Master the dimensions. Know your surroundings like you know your heartbeat. Build your strategy like the Creator built the world, with order, space, and divine purpose."
As the final wave of drills hit, something internal shifted.
A deeper clarity formed. A bond rose like a tide.
They were seeing things from different angles. Like the flow of service, defensive and offensive maneuvers also had different angles. They were looking and moving in all directions.
Not just fighters. Fellow heirs of a cause. They trained for hours until everyone began to see it more clearly. They were taking a short break, and then, the doors hissed open.
A new pulse filled the room. The light shifted. The very air trembled with quiet power.

Dr. E and Dr. Zayler had returned. Floating beside them, a hovering table glided forward, silent and smooth, carrying something radiant. Cubes. Small, glowing, and alive with power. Swirling arcs of light danced across their surfaces. Energy that seemed to hum with purpose, like whispers of creation encoded in design. Dr. E's voice cut through the quiet.
"I hope we're not interrupting anything important...
Because this changes everything."

The team instinctively gathered around. No one needed prompting.

They felt it in their core. This was the moment.

"These," Dr. Zayler added, "are the symbiotic cubes. Final stage. Fully keyed. We added a final touch. Each cube has a quiet voice, repeating the Word of God, claiming scripture. They were designed for one thing: resonance with purpose. They'll amplify your suit... but only if your heart is ready."

Dr. E nodded, her voice dropping to a sacred hush.

"Choose yours. Please insert it into the belt's center module. We do this together as one. On my count."

Each team member reached forward.

Fingers brushed the radiant cubes, warm with power, almost pulsing like heartbeats.

A shared breath. A charged stillness.

"One..." "Two..." "Three." Click.

The cubes snapped into place.

And the room lit up like a bright star.

Rays of light surged through their suits, arcs of energy traced across their arms, chests, and visors. Their nano-suits absorbed the cubes in their belts. The Synchronium itself responded, glowing to life in sync with their resonance.

Their armor shimmered. Their bond deepened.

Their calling intensified.

And though the cubes hummed with power...

It was the Light already within them, planted by their Creator, that made them whole. The bond between them crystallized and refined in trials, forged in Truth.

They were no longer just Team TIDES.

They were resurgent stewards.

They had found the core signal, a beacon of hope.

And it wasn't just the cubes.

They were carriers of light in a darkening world.

And the battle was about to change.

James stepped up to the holographic console, ready to initiate the next phase of training. But his fingers hovered over the interface a beat too long. Then, with a flick of his wrist, he shut it down.

He turned to the group. "What if we shake this up and take it outside? Real-world terrain. We've done enough in controlled space. Let's see what this gear does under the sun and sky where it counts."

No hesitation. No objections.

Just a surge of energy as the team moved as one toward the exit. The doors of the Forge opened wide and met the wild. They launched into the open, their suits adapting instantly to wind, terrain, and temperature. Every tree, breeze, and ripple of light felt sharper. Quicker. Tuned. They could resonate with creation and sense that it was fine-tuned. Their suits sang in the correct key, and creation was declaring God's power.

Each member instinctively shifted into their favorite mode. Zane caught the windstream first, vaulting over a rocky incline, wings and stabilizers unfurling from his back in a seamless construct.

"Okay," he shouted, grinning wide, "this just got real."

Tad hit the ground running, microspikes flaring from his boots as he gripped uneven terrain with ease. "Traction modulation dialed in an instant!" Puck called out, "Pods of three! Test against varied terrain!" The team scattered like clockwork up trees, over ridges, through dense brush, and open fields.

James reached for a slope, TENDRILs launched like muscle memory, pulling him upward.

"Confirmed: reflex latency gone. This system is reacting like a neural network." Dr. E confirmed, "That's how design works!"

Ryan and Brox ran a fast-paced sim drill, deploying decoys, multiple constructs, protective barriers, and sonic disruptors in layered, fluid arcs.

Then Dr. E's voice came through comms:
"Frogman Mode. Deploy and descend."
The pivot was seamless.
The team sprinted toward the lake, suits shifting into
hydromorphic configuration, and launched into the deep.
The symbiotic cores flexed with fluid precision.
Frogman Mode was alive.
They sliced through the trench, sonars lighting their HUDs in
layered pulses, amplified by lateral lines in schools of fish.
Puck slipped behind reeds, his suit adjusting color and
movement, blending with the underwater foliage.
The Heart Cores pulsed faint vibrations, reading the flow,
interpreting direction, and intention.
They moved like currents through the water.
Smooth. Purposeful. Unified.
Then Puck gave the signal.
"Surface and return to Frogman Bay!"
They angled upward, thrusting to the surface.
Together, they vaulted through the tunnel into the Vaultrium's
re-entry bay, landing in formation.
Tad exhaled, laughing. "Okay... that was next-level."
Ryan nodded. "And we're not even scratching the surface."
Their armor still shimmered. But something deeper had
awakened.
They weren't just connected by tech.
They were aligned by rhythm. By purpose. By a design that
could only come from one place.
They carried a light that wasn't forged in any lab.
It was placed in them by their Creator.
They had chosen not to fight that truth, but to align with it.
And by using sound science, they had studied the world,
mirrored its design, and learned how to act, not react. This is
how intelligent minds study the environment and learn from
the system that already works.

Nothing about their progress was accidental. You can't wait to adapt when darkness accelerates. Excellence doesn't appear by chance—it's crafted. Dr. E used her mind with intention; design always reflects a designer. Team TIDES wasn't an accident; they were an answer. Dr. E designed the suit with purpose, and the team stepped into that purpose, preparing ahead for the challenges they knew would come. Readiness is built long before the moment demands it.

Later that evening, the team gathered around the Halo HUD for a final debrief. The energy in the room had shifted—focused, steady, aware of what was coming next.

They planned.
They trained.
They had synced.
Now it was time to divide.
Not in spirit, but in mission.

They reviewed the differences in the new technology. It was like solving a problem from every angle. They had learned not to get stuck in a tunnel but to cover the entire field, each from a different vantage point. Sometimes you just need the right tool—or the right perspective—to overcome. Two things never solve a crisis: using the wrong tool or waiting for one to be invented after it's too late.

That's why this team was ready.
They weren't just armored.
They were equipped with intelligence and heart. As the darkness was spreading, and responding to their actions to try and stop the spreading of the light. It was time to make intelligent connections and find those to join the mission to confront the rise of RIPTIDE's schemes.

To overcome the enemy, they would need to study the shifting battlefield, adapt with strategy, and build alliances that extended beyond their team.

Working with the symbiotic cores wasn't about worshiping nature as some divine force; it was about honoring the Creator who designed it, modeling design after functional abilities.

God had entrusted mankind with the role of stewardship, not submission to creation. They weren't called to serve creation, but to govern it correctly.

It would take trust, discernment... and faith that God would guide their every step.

Mr. Hardee stepped forward. His voice was calm, but full of gravity.

"Team TIDES, we've come a long way. But we're not done. To move forward, I'll be taking volunteers to build partnerships, share intelligence, lean on trust, and walk through doors only God can open or close.

The rest of you will pursue the artifacts and follow their trail. Stay sharp. Stay grounded.

We'll regroup when the time is right."

He paused, looking around the room.

"But tonight... we rest.

You've earned it. Hit the showers, take some downtime, and let's just be a team for a little while longer."

Jones perked up. "How about everyone come over to my place? Fire up the grills, get the firepit going, play some guitar, and hear what wild stories you all have to tell."

Luna threw her hands in the air. "Woo hoo! Now we're talkin'!"

Laughter broke out as the team nodded and agreed, already heading toward their quarters to clean up.

Tonight, they were more than warriors.
They were brothers, sisters, friends,
and a family on a mission.

# The Quest of the Keepers

The next morning carried the weight of both excitement and sadness. It was time to say goodbye, at least for now, to nearly half the team. The memories of the night before still lingered in their hearts: laughter around the fire, sing-alongs, wild theories, and heartfelt stories. They'd shared tales of the bottle found in the attic, the moonlit artifact, the airplane wing cross-section, the gear, the second bottle from the train, and the riddle etched in time. For the newest team members, it was more than just storytelling; it was an initiation into something bigger. And for those who had been on the journey since their youth, it was a reminder of how far they'd come.

That morning felt like an extension of last night's fellowship, with warm breakfast, shared smiles, and quiet moments of reflection.

Two paths lay ahead, but purpose bound them all: Teamwork. Integrity. Dedication. Excellence. Service. TIDES wasn't just a name. It was a mission etched on their hearts with the faith to do the work ahead.

The team departing on the quest for the "Keepers" gathered at the Forge entrance, exchanging farewells and blessings with those heading out to form new alliances and open doors of influence. The rest turned back inside, cleaned up, suited up, and circled the Halo Hub for final preparations.

On the table before them, every artifact lay carefully secured, each protected inside a soft, impact-resistant case, cushioned with high-tech gel to absorb shock and redistribute weight. Each case could be worn like a backpack, keeping hands free and hearts focused.

As one, the team recited the riddle again, both a clue and a call:
"The light of space stands tall in its place,
Rooted on earth, below the hands that trace,
The flow of time to guide the vessel,
That bears the weight of what truly matters.
Take with you what you have discovered,
For only together will the truth be uncovered."

James stepped forward, reviewing each known artifact for the benefit of the newer members. Puck followed, retelling Matt's story about the Keepers, guardians not just of lighthouses, but of time itself, through old clocks and hidden libraries.

Dr. E dimmed the lights, activating a holographic map of the town.

"This is our best match for the Keepers' Library," she said. "All signs point here, historical alignment, structural markers, and topographic cues from the artifact's map."

She scanned the room. "This is more than a field mission. This is legacy work."

No one had to speak; their eyes said it all.

It was time.

The Vaultrium bay doors slid open with a hydraulic hiss.

Inside was the team's transport arsenal, sleek, black-paneled walls glowing with cyan interface lights. A collection of vehicles shimmered beneath the overhead beams.

There were pulse-cycles with adaptive plating, zero-sound trail modes, and kinetic acceleration.

Among the vast equipment, there was also a multi-terrain truck equipped with climbing treads, retractable grapples, and undercarriage boosters.

Among the lineup, a silver sport cruiser with a silent stealth drive was an available option.

Puck raised an eyebrow, a grin spreading across his face. "Alright... now this feels like the right kind of field trip."

RaJohn walked up to the silver cruiser, running a hand along the hood. "This one's mine." James pointed at it with a smirk. "I call dibs on the way back."

Jones gave a low whistle as he circled a tanked-out black truck. It looked like it could scale a wall without breaking a sweat. "Built like a skyscraper crawler... yeah, this beast's coming with me."

Zane, Tad, and Puck beelined to the pulse-powered bikes. With silent starters and hyper-responsive handling, they felt more like extensions of the body than machines.

Then Luna crossed her arms, staring at the lineup. "Let me get this straight," she said, raising her voice. "I can fly in a suit, scale walls, and punch through concrete, but now I'm just a passenger again?"

She planted a hand on her hip with mock exasperation. "What am I, fourteen? Can't drive, but apparently I can fight global evil."

The room erupted in laughter.

Jones leaned over one of the truck's open control panels. "Well... you could ride with me. The back console's got a full ops deck. Scanner banks, holographic console, thermal satellite feeds, and it's synced to the Vaultrium's live comms. Basically, it's a mobile command center." Luna's eyes lit up. "Wait, do I get to run the scans?" "Full control," Jones said. "Thermal overlays, old building schematics, anomaly tracking... and you pick the playlist." She grinned. "I call shotgun. And I'm queuing up the music now."

Jones tipped an imaginary hat. "Hop in, Commander Luna."

Puck looked around the room. They weren't just gearing up; they were stepping into a legacy to leave behind.

And Luna? She was having the time of her life. She added that youthful love for all things pure, even with her brilliant mind.

The convoy slipped out of the Forge just as dawn bled into the sky. LED interface lights winked on across the vehicles, their silent hum blending with the whisper of shifting gears. Jones's tactical truck led the way, Luna's drones drifting above its roof like lanterns. Behind them, Tad, Zane, and Puck leaned into their pulse-powered cycles, visors alight with synced Holo-HUD data. RaJohn's silver cruiser hugged the asphalt as James perched beside him. The world unfurled before them in motion, rolling fields gilded by morning light, ribbons of river crossings, and wood-lined crests fading into distant pastures. The air shifted as they crested a final ridge. Ahead lay Beacon's Reach: a town of balanced ambition. Solar-glass roofs shimmered on brick-and-timber storefronts. Vintage trolleys clattered along cobbled streets, passing families at play in manicured parks and parishioners tending hedges around a grand stone church. Neon-white streetlamps blended old-world charm with discreet tech satchels for public Wi-Fi. Luna's console flashed: "Beacon's Reach-tech and tradition in harmony. Law enforcement is strong. Crime rate is minimal." The convoy coasted through the heart of the town, each member taking in the scene.

As the last fountain came into view, a roar erupted behind them, tires humming against pavement. Another silver sports car careened into their lane, sparks dancing where metal kissed concrete. Luna's calm voice cut through the comms: "Erratic driver, ten o'clock." Without breaking stride, Puck, Tad, and Zane launched sticky-net pods from their wrists. The pods bloomed across all four wheels of the sports car in an instant, yanking it to a halt. Puck and Tad each shot a dab of bio-gel at both door latches in perfect Sync Mode communication. Tad called over the roar of engines, "Easy there, partner-care to explain yourself to this officer?" As the local police cruiser slid in by the suspect, Team TIDES saluted and pulled away, as their vehicles moved back into formation.

Beyond Beacon's Reach, the night fell. The road dipped into Duskwatch Hollow. Once a sister city, it now sprawls with stacked warehouses, neon-lit clubs, and digital billboards hawking every vice. Luna's drones captured thermal clusters in dingy alleyways; James's HUD flagged high-crime zones. Bars glowed, their patrons swaying beneath trash-strewn street lamps. RaJohn murmured, "Innovation here became idol worship. They bank on distraction, not community. A little leven, levens the whole lump." Puck added quietly, "Where growth and community once stood, they now kneel before status." Luna's fingers keyed in on her console. "Multiple armed suspects reported ahead. Local PD is out-manned and out-gunned."

The team formed a tight line near the police barricade. Dr. E's voice crackled through their comms: "Team TIDES inbound to assist the officers on scene, stand by for our link." Jones killed his engine. Luna's drones wheeled overhead, casting flickering shadows. Puck's tone sharpened:

"Luna, thermal Overwatch. James and RaJohn will flank from the west. Jones, Zane, meet the sergeant at the blockade. Tad and I will take the high-rise entry for vantage."

Shadows stretched long across Duskwatch Hollow. Beacon's Reach had shown them harmony; here, they beheld the cost of abandoning Truth. Now, shoulder to shoulder with local law enforcement, they were prepared to bring light into darkness.

"Let's use our tech for good," Puck called out. He and Tad vaulted into the air, their suits shifting into Frogman RGM.

Each landed silently on opposite rooftops. Jones strode forward, hands raised. "Sergeant, we're here to assist." The weary officer glanced up, relief flooding his features. "Great, saw you on the news. Glad you showed." Before he could continue, Luna interjected, "Hold position: thermal shows four targets."

Dr. E's voice crackled in their ears as she pulled up a wider satellite thermal sweep. "Wide feed looks clear so far, team," she reported. Luna keyed her console. "Puck and Tad, two perps in that alley, hostage in their grip. Fourth target's holed up inside the northern storage room." James's visor highlighted the figures. "Sounds like a dropshipping hub for hot tech. The sergeant says they've been stealing the latest gear straight off the market."

The sergeant's voice came through: "They've ripped off every tech dealer in town; nobody's safe. Victims end up running empty-handed... or worse."

High on the rooftops, Puck and Tad readied themselves. Puck's voice rang out over comms, clipped and clear: "James, RaJohn-deploy decoy projections to draw their gaze at the alley mouth and generate a shield around the hostage. Jones and Zane ghosted in through the side entrance. Tad and I will neutralize the pair out front. Secure the hostage first, then give us the cue."

"Copy that," James replied. He and RaJohn slipped into Stealth Mode, advancing along the building's shadowed flank. Holographic decoys flickered into view behind them, drawing the perps' aim. RaJohn deployed a construct wall of shielding between the perps and the hostage. At Puck's signal, both he and Tad fired TENDRILs, whipping through the air, snatching rifles clean from their hands. Simultaneously, James and RaJohn unleashed sonic pulses that sent the hoodlums stumbling back against the brick wall.

Tad dropped from his perch, landing precisely beside Puck. Together, they bound the pair in sticky TENDRIL cuffs, both subjects with stable vitals. The alley fell silent. Inside, the fourth perp crept toward a window, curious about the commotion. But James and RaJohn anticipated the move, goo pods exploded at his feet, instantly immobilizing him. As their suits phased back to normal mode, the man stared in disbelief.

Under the neon glow of Duskwatch Hollow, Team TIDES regrouped with the sergeant and his officers. The perp, still stunned, managed, "I-I've been nabbed by the TIDES guys on TV at the senate hearing. Are you kidding me?"

Puck stepped forward, "No joke," he said, voice steady. "You're done here."

The sergeant cracked a grin. "Will you be in town all week? We've got openings every night here in Duskwatch."

The team laughed. Puck shook his head. "Sorry, we're bound for Port of Valor. We've got some digging into our team's history to do. Can we take a rain check?"

"Yes. Valor is awesome," the sergeant said. "That's where I live. I love its history. It's been passed down for generations with a purpose. If you need a place big enough for all of you, my aunt Rose runs the local inn: The Gilded Lantern. Should I tell her to expect you?" Puck exchanged glances with the team, a smile tugging at his lips. "Please do. We'll see you in Valor."

They climbed into their vehicles once more. Duskwatch Hollow slipped into their rearview mirrors. Within minutes, the oppressive tension lifted, the air grew crisper, and the moon cast light across rolling fields. A brisk sea breeze carried the tang of salt and the soft sweetness of jasmine drifting down from cliffside gardens.

On either side of the winding coastal road, centuries-old stone buildings stood resolute, their lanterns now flickering to life, casting dancing patterns on cobblestones. Manicured gardens framed quaint churches and boutique storefronts, each edifice whispering tales of generations past.

Rounding a cliff-side bend, their headlights swept across the first beam of the lighthouse, cutting through dusk, its sentinel glow rotating in measured arcs high above the adjacent headland. Then, tucked against the curve of a sheltered cove, they spotted it: an antiqued, polished brass sign above the door, 'The Gilded Lantern Inn.'

The Inn stood like a timeless memory at the edge of the cove, its ivy-strewn stone walls glowing gold in the rays of lamp posts. Above the arched entryway, a carefully crafted compass rose had been etched into the keystone. Beneath it, two inscriptions flanked the doorway:

"Set your course by the Light that never fades."

"Let Truth be your guide through every storm."


The words gleamed faintly in the light, like promises. Carrying their artifact cases with reverent caution, the team approached the door. Embedded into the weathered oak was an ornate emblem: an octopus curled around a full moon, its limbs poised mid-motion as if alive. The air shifted, cooler, heavier, meaningful. A quiet tingle ran down each team member's spine. Puck stepped forward to knock, but before his hand touched the oak, the door creaked open.

"Welcome... welcome. Come on in, come in, come in," came the warm voice from within.

A woman stood in the threshold, poised but kind, ageless in a way that made you wonder if she'd seen more than she let on. Her hair was as silver as the moon, and she wore sea-glass earrings. Her eyes sparkled like sunlight on saltwater.

"I've been expecting you," she smiled. "So glad you're here." As the team stepped inside, a large dog and a sleek cat padded in from the back hall, tails lifted with curiosity. The interior of the inn was a wonder: an elegant fusion of old-world craftsmanship and forward-thinking innovation. Wood-paneled walls carried the scent of lavender and sea salt, while subtle holoscreens flickered between ancient brass lanterns. Nautical maps hung beside touch-sensitive display glass. Time layered upon time, effortless, intentional.

The dog wagged enthusiastically, nosing Jones and Zane's hands. The cat wove around Luna and Puck, its eyes wide, glowing faintly in the lantern light.

"Wow," Luna laughed, bending down to pet the feline. "Your cat and dog are really friendly."

"Oh, I hope none of you are allergic," Rose chuckled, ruffling the dog's ears. "That's Needle," she said, nodding toward the cat. "And this is Rudder." She gently turned the dog's tail like a ship's tiller. "They've been with me longer than I can remember. They're harmless... unless you're carrying bad intentions." She paused, then smiled. "Animals see what we often miss. They don't just look at you, they read your presence. The fact that they've taken to you so quickly? That says everything."

"They're incredible," said Luna softly.

"Come now, let me show you to your rooms," Rose gestured, stepping toward a richly carved hallway. "But first, the guest book."

At the base of a wide staircase, in front of the fireplace, stood a low wooden coffee table, smooth mahogany wrapped in brass cornering, carved with maritime sigils and fine etchings of constellations. Resting atop it was a leather-bound book, its cover tooled with the same compass rose as above the door. A feather quill rested in an inkwell beside it.

"Write your names, all of you," Rose instructed gently. "This book has held every worthy traveler who's ever passed through Valor's gate. It's more than tradition, it's a connection."

Each team member approached the book in turn. When Puck dipped the quill into the ink and pressed it to the page, he felt something shift. Like a gust catching a sail. As Luna scrolled her name in precise strokes, the room quieted, almost reverently.

One by one, the others followed.

It wasn't just a signature.

It was an invitation. A welcoming. A moment that sealed them to the town, and perhaps to its deeper mysteries.

As the final name dried on the parchment, Needle leapt onto the edge of the table, tail flicked, then took off down a shadowy corridor that led toward the back of the inn.

Rudder gave a soft chuff, ears perked, then padded after Needle. Rose just smiled.

"They know this place better than anyone," she said. "Don't be surprised if they lead you somewhere unexpected."

She motioned down the hall, guiding the team to their rooms. After everyone found a cozy space to settle in, she paused once more. "Join me for a hot meal in the dining hall, just down to the left when you're ready. Everything should be nearly finished. I know you must be hungry after what happened in the Hollow. My nephew told me everything when he called ahead to say you were coming." Her smile softened. "Thank you for helping him. That meant more than you know. It will come back to you before you know it."

With a graceful nod, she turned the corner and disappeared into the warm light at the end of the corridor.

The team lingered quietly for a moment, each stepping into their assigned rooms. The doors creaked open to reveal spaces full of warmth and heritage: maritime relics, carved driftwood beams, storm lanterns, and high arched ceilings like the ribs of a great wooden ship. It felt less like a hotel and more like a memory, something familiar and sacred.

Puck stepped inside his room and exhaled slowly.

He set his backpack down and moved to the wash basin to rinse his face. Cool water ran through his fingers like threads of the past meeting the present. He looked up into the mirror and stared at his reflection.

Then, he heard it—the rain.

Soft at first, like a whisper against the hull of a ship.

He turned toward the small, round window above the sink, a perfect porthole, fogging slightly with the warmth inside. The glass caught the glow of a lantern outside as raindrops traced quiet lines down the pane, one drawing its own path, flowing and merging with the next.

A small grin found its way to Puck's mouth.

This moment was familiar, like the first chapter in his life.
He'd once sat by a rain-streaked window as a young boy,
dreaming of sea turtles and sunken cities. Of hidden treasure
and underwater tunnels. Of a world below the surface waiting
to be explored. That memory hadn't left him. It had grown with
him, and the drops of rain were merging again.
He placed a hand against the cool glass.
The rain outside now seemed to fall with purpose, not just as
weather, but as a gentle reminder of what brings life. The soil
needs it. The trees need it. So do we.
His heart stirred.
And there, in the silence, the words of Christ came back to him,
not from a textbook, not from a briefing or lecture, but from
the place where Truth writes itself into the soul:
"I Am the Living Water." Puck closed his eyes.
A wave of reverence washed over him. The weight of
everything, the mission, the timing, the connections, settled
like the calm after a storm. None of this was a coincidence.
Every step, every moment, every detour had been purposeful.
God had not only opened the way... He had walked it with
them.
Puck whispered a quiet prayer.
"Thank you for guiding us. For bringing us this far. For not
letting go, even when I didn't know what I was reaching for."
He opened his eyes and looked again through the porthole.
The rain shimmered in the golden glow of the lanterns outside.
Needle darted past the hall, tail flicking. Rudder followed
behind.
And in that small, quiet moment, everything felt connected.
Puck's eyes remained wide with wonder. Because when the
path is lit from above, even the rain becomes part of the
journey. There are too many moments in life, too perfectly
timed, too deeply meaningful, for anyone with eyes truly open,
to believe they're just chance.

With the team gathered in the dining hall, they pitched in to help Rose set the long table, carrying over steaming platters and clinking dishes filled with coastal flavor. The air was rich with the scent of herbs, firewood, and slow-cooked memories. The front door creaked open, letting in the faintest trace of salt air. Heavy boots echoed across the wooden floorboards.

"Elias, come wash up, dinner's ready," Rose called warmly.

"I could smell that Frogmore stew from halfway down the lane," came the voice from the foyer.

Puck turned toward the doorway. "Sarge? Elias, right? Good to meet you outside Duskwatch Hollow."

They shook hands.

"You heard right," Elias said, grinning. "Frogmore stew, don't let the name scare you. No frogs. Just potatoes, sausage, shrimp, corn, clams... and Aunt Rose's seasoning legends."

"I also smell chowder," Luna added, smiling at Rose.

"And hush puppies. And oyster pie. And probably a dozen other things we haven't discovered yet," RaJohn said, eyes wide.

Rose waved them toward their seats with a humble shrug. "It's no trouble at all. Cooking for a crew with purpose? That's a privilege."

As they settled in around the long table, Rose stepped forward again and held out both hands.

"Before we take a single bite," she said gently, "let's thank the One who brought us this far."

They all reached for one another's hands, as a circle formed around the table.

With quiet reverence, Rose bowed her head. "Father, thank You for this food, for these hands, and for the unseen ways You guide our steps. May this place be a rest stop for the weary, a beacon for the searching, and a shelter for those walking in Your light. Bless this team, their mission, and the path ahead. In Jesus' name, amen."

"Amen," the team echoed softly.

Then came the passing of plates, the clatter of silverware, and the kind of laughter that only rises when bellies and hearts are both full.

Elias leaned back in his chair with a grin. "So... what brings you to Valor? Feels like more than just a road trip."

Puck paused, thoughtful. "Let's just say, we're chasing pieces of something. Clues. Fragments. And maybe a bit of history, if it's willing to be found." Rose tilted her head slightly. "This town's seen its fair share of those."

Zane glanced up. "Any clues?"

Rose smiled faintly, not answering directly. "Port of Valor was always more than docks and trade. Folks lived off the sea, but their minds were sharp. They built various things, including metalwork, glass, and even early forms of technology. They believed in using it to help people. God gives us tools, but it is up to us to use them for good and find new ways to use them using sound science."

"Sounds like they were ahead of their time," Tad said.

"They were," Elias added gently. "Sometimes the world catches up. Sometimes it doesn't. But Valor's always known how to hold its ground. If the people here did anything, it had purpose and a meaning behind it."

The fire popped quietly in the hearth.

Rose's eyes lingered on Puck. "You said your name was Puck?"

He nodded, lowering his spoon.

"You wouldn't happen to be related to an old diver named Eben, would you? Eben Puck, I believe?"

Puck blinked. "That was my great-great-grandfather's name."

A soft smile curled on Rose's lips. "I thought so. He came through Valor often. Said this town was... how did he put it? 'A quiet compass for the noisy world.' He stayed here, in this very inn." The table fell still. Something unspoken hung in the air.

"What did he do here?" James asked quietly.

Rose began collecting bowls. "He helped build things, fix things, and he dove along the coast in the mid-1900s, sometimes farther. Left behind more than most folks ever knew. But he wasn't the only one. Folks from that generation didn't hoard much. They gave. They served. They lived light, but deep."

Puck's voice softened. "He passed long before I was born. Not much was left of his things. I don't know much. But I've always had the feeling... he was part of something more."

Rose nodded, her expression unreadable at first.

Then, before disappearing into the kitchen, she paused beside a photo frame hanging on the wall. Her fingers brushed the wooden edge as she glanced back.

"He left you more than you know," she said gently. "Some gifts don't go on a shelf-or in a bank. Some are sewn into your heart." She pointed toward a young man in the photo, broad-shouldered, full head of brown hair, wearing a sailor's jacket and a quiet smile that somehow felt familiar.

"That's him, and his jacket," she added. "Right there. Standing proud. Quiet. But watchful. Just like you." Puck turned toward the picture, something catching in his chest. His gaze locked on the man's eyes, and for the first time, it felt like the pieces weren't just falling into place; they were rising to meet him.

"Feels like we were meant to come here," Luna whispered.

RaJohn nodded slowly. "Feels like someone left the light on for us."

The team helped clean up from dinner and gathered in the living room around the fireplace. The storm outside had passed, and moonlight now spilled through the high windows, casting silver rays across the floor. The fire crackled as they settled into chairs and cushions. The walls seemed to hum with stories waiting to be told. Elias showed himself to the door, then turned back. "I leave you in good hands," he said with a half-smile. "Good night." "Good night, Sarge," They called out.

The door clicked shut behind him. Inside, the Gilded Lantern felt like more than a place to sleep. It felt like a beginning. Though the day had been long, the hour was still early, and the inn whispered with stories yet untold. Something hung in the air, an energy, a beckoning, as if they were on the edge of a deeper discovery. They all felt it.

In the hallway behind them, silent as a shadow, Needle slipped down the corridor, tail held high, guiding the way. Needle padded softly up to Puck, circled once, then leapt into his lap, purring. She kneaded her paws on his stomach with all the seriousness of a baker at dawn.

The team chuckled. "Needle really likes you," Tad said with a grin. Then, just as quickly, the cat jumped down and turned in a circle. She meowed once, trotted a few paces, then glanced back over her shoulder, waiting.

"Okay, okay," Puck said, rising. "I get it. I'm coming."

He followed the feline down a side hall, deeper into the inn. The rest of the team exchanged looks and fell in behind him. Needle led them into a quiet, large library, book-lined room warmed by low lamp light and the faint scent of cedar and salt.

The cat darted between two tall shelves and disappeared into a shadowed crevice. Puck looked at the wall and saw a plate with an octopus emblem that had the inscription, "By way of the Keeper's Tides." He crouched and reached toward the narrow gap. A cool draft brushed his fingertips. He stood again, looking around the shelves. Then something caught his eye: a lantern above the plaque, gilded and aged, its base mounted to the wall. The metal arc at its base had a barely visible groove —a curved mark that lined up perfectly with a matching etching on the lamp's base. Puck reached out, resting his fingers along the groove. Slowly, he twisted the lantern, turning it in the direction of the grooves on the base.

Click.

The bookshelf shifted. A whisper of air escaped as it popped free from the wall, swinging outward like a door.

Behind it, darkness. And stone.

A narrow staircase curved down into the unknown, guarded by an old oak handrail smoothed by time.

Puck took a step back and called out, "Aunt Rose, you might want to see this." The other team members stared in wonder.

Footsteps padded quickly from the hall.

Rose stopped in the doorway, her eyes going wide, not in surprise, but in memory.

Puck looked from her to the stairwell. "What do you make of this?"

Rose approached, gently placing a hand on the doorframe. Her voice was soft, but full of meaning.

"If you seek, you will find. Knock, and the door will be opened to you." She met Puck's eyes. "You know, everything unfolds in its time... for those who seek Him. Only those who ask will receive. And this," she looked down the steps, "this is a path for seekers. This is the quest you're on."

Her words settled over them like a warm wind before a storm. Puck turned back to the stairs, heart pounding, not with fear, but with purpose. They had followed the Light this far.

Now, it was time to go deeper.

Just inside the stairwell, another lantern hung crookedly on the wall. Puck reached up and turned it upright. Instantly, the flame ignited, and one by one, more lanterns came to life, each casting warm light on the stone path ahead.

The team moved in close behind him as they descended. The stairs wound downward, then abruptly curved upward again, carrying them higher than where they had started. At last, the passage opened into a vast chamber built into the rock. It felt old, ancient even, but also built with care and precision. Purpose filled the space and their hearts as they looked around searching for answers.

Dust hung in the air like the breath of time.

And there, perched casually atop a table, was Needle.

She flicked her tail and blinked slowly at them, like she'd been waiting all along.

Puck stepped forward, still scanning the room.

There was a large metal door on one wall. Beside the door was a large, circular emblem, an octopus, its tentacles curling outward, but the top portion was incomplete. There was only an empty socket, shaped unmistakably like twin wings.

Directly beside the metal door was an opening that looked out into the night.

This huge window rested atop a short stack of stairs, framing the lighthouse, tall and watchful, its light slowly sweeping across the cliffs.

Another opening pointed to a nearby clock tower, standing beside a church capped with a wooden cross. The team took it all in, breaths held.

Symbols. Artifacts. Purpose.

Something was beginning to align.

Puck stepped closer to the emblem, voice low. "This... this is just the first key." He turned to Zane. "The airplane artifact, do you have it?" Zane nodded, activated his watch, and blurred out of sight. He returned seconds later, suit retracting, the artifact case cradled in his arms.

Puck opened the case carefully, eyes narrowing as he studied the object. The stylized octopus on the wall... the artifact in his hands... something matched. He twisted the cross sections of the airplane wings gently, and with a soft click, they detached from the top of the figure like puzzle pieces. He approached the emblem, found the socket, and slid the wings into place.

They locked in with a satisfying thunk.

Everyone waited.

A breath.

Two.

133

Puck tried turning the emblem. Nothing. He pressed it, still nothing. He stepped back, brow furrowed, eyes drifting again toward the windows. The lighthouse. The clock tower. Two anchors in a sea of mystery.

Across the room, James caught his gaze.

And together, the word fell from their lips like a spark catching flame:

"Teamwork. Together."

Puck nodded, a plan already forming. "We're close. Let's suit up. Record the feed and send it to the Vaultrium Hub. Dr. E and the others should see this." The team activated their suits with practiced ease. Armor slid into place, visors locked, and lights pulsed in synchronized rhythm. Dr. E's face blinked into view on their displays. "Signal received. I'm watching. What is this place?" "We found a hidden chamber," Puck replied. "An octopus emblem with missing cross-sections of the wings. It matches the airplane artifact. Windows are pointing to the lighthouse and the clock tower. We think each place corresponds to one of the artifacts."

Jones stepped forward. "The gear cog belongs in the clock tower. Mechanical precision." "And the moonlit artifact has to be the lighthouse," RaJohn said. "Symbolic. Literal. It's all there."

Tad nodded. "That leaves the ship-in-a-bottle and the octopus emblem. They're next..." Puck looked to Zane. "Flight station is yours." Zane gave a confident nod. "Copy that. Needle and I got this."

Needle walked up the steps to look out the window, her fur catching the moonlight like woven silver. The team moved quietly through the Gilded Lantern's wide hallways, boots soft against the polished wood. Before exiting, they paused in the main foyer, where Aunt Rose stood drying her hands on a dish towel. Puck gave her a grateful smile. "We're on the right track, Rose. We'll be back as soon as we can."

She nodded knowingly. "Follow the path as it's lit. Rudder, Needle, and I will keep the lights on. And don't miss the quiet parts along the way."

The team retrieved the remaining artifacts from their rooms. With that, they stepped onto the moonlit porch and into the evening air. Outside, the Port of Valor stretched wide and glowing beneath a thousand stars.

Luna and Jones exchanged a quick nod. Their flight modules hissed open. Micro-thrusters flared. Together, they launched, vaulting into the sky with silent propulsion, arcing smoothly toward the massive clock tower nestled beside the chapel.

RaJohn and James activated their frogman dive forms, sleek and nimble. They vanished down a side slope and into the water, racing toward the sea cliffs where the lighthouse waited like a beacon through generations.

That left Tad and Puck.

Their suits morphed into enhanced amphibious RGM. The towering chapel loomed ahead as they dashed in HRAM, its white-washed stone foundation rooted in rock like something historical. The rooftop would be a perfect vantage point.

"Ready?" Tad asked, rolling his shoulders.

"Let's go," Puck answered.

They leapt forward, agile and silent, crossing the courtyard in long, fluid strides. Within seconds, they were scaling the side of the chapel with practiced ease, their suits adapting seamlessly to the incline. Puck reached the base of the cross; Tad perched nearby, the whole port unfolded before them. The turning lamp from the lighthouse, the glowing face of the clock tower, the moon, the sea, and the pieces of a story coming together at last. Puck addressed Tad, "Time, space, and matter are a trinity. Without the three in place at once, nothing in the natural world could exist. Length, height, width. Past, present, future. Solid, liquid, gas. Trinities within trinities. All of it is an intentional design. A quest for Truth. This is our path."

Far below, Rose stood on the porch, lantern in hand, watching, waiting, and remembering.

"Just like the old days, with a bit more style," she whispered. Then she turned back inside, faithfully keeping the lights on. High above the Port of Valor, Jones and Luna touched down on an outer catwalk of the towering clocktower. The metal platform creaked under their weight as they made their way to a side entrance and slipped inside. The interior was breathtaking. It was a cathedral of gears, pendulums, and precision, each piece a tribute to craftsmanship long past. Polished brass gleamed in the low light, and the rhythmic ticking of perfectly timed gears echoed through the chamber. Jones, eyes bright, couldn't help but admire it. "They don't make them like this anymore," he said, voice low with awe.

"It's keeping perfect time," Luna observed, scanning the walls. "So where does the gear artifact fit in?"

"Look for a symbol," Jones replied. "An octopus... a gear... something that marks the spot."

They moved carefully, descending a few flights and checking each landing. Finally, at the base, just below the main clock chamber, Luna spotted it. A metal panel inset into the wall beside a metal door, identical in design to the one they'd discovered in the hidden library room. Next to it, a circular indentation. It was the unmistakable outline of the gear artifact.

"Guys, are you seeing this?" Luna said into the comms. "We found it." "Roger that," came RaJohn's voice. "James and I just reached the rocks at the base of the lighthouse."

Jones unlatched his pack and carefully removed the artifact. The polished gear shimmered as he aligned it with the slot and pressed it into place. Click.

But just like before, nothing.

It didn't turn. Didn't press inward. It locked into place, inert.

"Same situation here," Luna reported. "It won't budge-just like the first one."

The Halo HUD flickered to life again. Dr. E, Celeste, and Shonté are now fully tuned in on the comms.

"You guys know the suspense is killing us, right?" Celeste grinned.

"But you've got this," Shonté added. "You're so close. Keep going!"

At the lighthouse, James and RaJohn climbed carefully over slick rocks and washed-up driftwood until they reached the heavy door at its base. It groaned open under their hands, revealing a narrow spiral staircase coiled tightly up through the ancient stone tower.

No keeper. No voices. Just the soft whir of the turning light above.

They exchanged a glance and started up the steps.

At the top, the sound of gentle wind greeted them like an old friend. The panoramic view was breathtaking. The waves were crashing on the outer seawall, moonlight gilding the endless ocean, and the crisp air brimming with quiet wonder.

But their eyes stayed sharp, no time to linger.

They circled the rotating beacon, scanning every brace, every seam, every carving.

"We're looking for a symbol," James said, moving cautiously. "Moon... light... something."

RaJohn nodded, unzipping his gel-sealed pack and carefully withdrawing the moonlit artifact. "It's got to be here somewhere. We just have to find the keyhole."

James paused, glancing upward.

Just beneath the massive rotating lens, a secondary ring slowly spun in tandem, etched faintly with symbols. One of them made his breath catch: a full moon casting light over a ship's bow, guiding it toward safe harbor.

Click.

James froze. "Did you hear that?"

Click.

They both heard it again, soft, mechanical, and rhythmic.

"It's coming from the other side-near the south harbor," RaJohn said, already circling the top balcony. Then he spotted it.

"There," he pointed. "That flap on the second ring. It opens for one full rotation. Look."

Click. The panel slid open just long enough to expose a recessed compartment, then closed again.

James readied the artifact. "We time it right. Insert it mid-cycle."

They waited, tense. Moonlight shimmered across the lens. The panel slid open again.

James stepped forward with precision and fit the moonlit artifact into the cradle-shaped slot inside the rotating mechanism.

Click.

Whirrrr-ka-thunk.

It locked into place with a satisfying finality.

The second ring's rotation slowed... then stopped in a precise location and brightened.

It created a second beam of the lighthouse, casting its full brilliance on a distant section of the harbor, one that had been cloaked in darkness.

Below the surface, faint outlines glimmered; something was submerged. Something waiting.

RaJohn leaned forward, breath caught. "It's not just guiding ships anymore... It's guiding us."

On the rooftop of the chapel, Tad and Puck clung to opposite sides of the towering cross. From their vantage point, they could see the lighthouse beam piercing the water.

Puck scanned through his visor. "Looks like a tunnel entrance... just below the surface. You ready?"

They launched TENDRIL grapples, deploying with precision, wrapping around the frame of the cross. The two soared briefly through the night air, arcing like twin shadows across the moonlit sky, before rappelling smoothly down the side of the chapel and landing clean on the stone courtyard below. Without hesitation, they sprinted toward the water's edge. In one seamless motion, they plunged into the harbor and vanished beneath the waves.

Below, the lighthouse beam cut through the murk like a blade of truth, illuminating the arched opening of a tunnel carved into the seawall.

Puck activated his comms. "Dr. E... we've found the entrance." He and Tad swam inside, the tunnel eerily quiet, but somehow familiar. They surfaced into an open cavern, and moonlight shone from above, casting its glow onto a stone chamber. The beam revealed a metal door set into the rock, marked with the same octopus symbol they'd seen before.

They rushed to insert the octopus artifact. Again, nothing happened.

"We still have the bottle," Tad said, lifting it carefully. "Where does that fit in? It has a ship on it."

Puck stepped back, thinking. "Wait... The door you seek and find, the light guides the path. Narrow... time, space, matter, all have to be present, a trinity within a trinity. Teamwork for TIDES and together."

He activated the comm. "Everyone, pull out your artifacts. Let's insert them at the same time. Keep the moonlit one out. Gear. Wings. Octopus. Lock in sync. Ready? One... two... three." Click. Each artifact slid into place. Click.

They rotated 180 degrees in unison. Click.

The doors cracked open with a hiss of air, old seals breaking like the breath of time.

# -The Trinity Keys-

"James, RaJohn, might as well join us," Puck said. "Bring the artifacts. I have a feeling we're all about to see each other." Within minutes, each team member arrived through the newly opened doorway, stepping into a corridor lit by a trail of gilded lanterns. Their warm glow guided the way like beacons, leading into a central chamber, vast, circular, and awe-inspiring. The room felt like a cathedral carved from the heart of the earth, ancient and purposeful. Near one metal door, stood two stone pedestals. One held a lantern, flickering quietly. The other bore the engraved symbol of a ship, elegant and unmistakable. Across from them loomed a final locked door, its surface inlaid with the intricate emblems of the octopus, the moon, and a cluster of interlocking gears. Flanking the hallway they'd just entered were four smaller doors, each marked with one of the original artifact symbols: the moon, the octopus, a gear, and the wings of flight. Their brass handles, aged but polished, turned easily; they were already unlocked. Inside those chambers, the team discovered what could only be described as laboratories of legacy. Ingenious designs lined the walls. There was early frogman diving gear, advanced aviation schematics, mechanical prototypes, and other animal-inspired engineering. Diagrams and sketches revealed a clear pattern: a generation devoted not to conquering nature, but to studying it, learning from it, and stewarding its wonders. Creation, observed with reverence, repurposed for good.

After taking in the craftsmanship and vision around them, the team returned to the central pedestal. Puck carefully removed the bottle from his pack and placed it on the pedestal with the ship emblem. It had been a while, but he'd seen this before.

Then, the lantern light poured through the glass bottle, casting shimmering refractions that danced across the stone. The beam split into three precise rays, each one falling

...on a single cobblestone embedded in the wall, forming a perfect triangle of light-like stars etched on an ancient map. Puck's voice fell to a whisper. "The attic... it nearly shattered. All that time ago..."

Tad nodded, eyes never leaving the glowing stones. "It's always been part of the design. Fragile. Purposeful. And perfectly timed."

Together, they stepped toward the wall. With care, they pulled the three illuminated stones free. Behind them, a hidden compartment slid open, revealing three flat metallic keys- simple, elegant, and engraved with a single word each:

Time. Space. Matter.

Puck, Tad, and Zane each took one, the cool weight of the metal grounding them in the moment.

"One last lock," Puck said quietly. "Together."

They turned them in unison.

Click. Whirrrr. Click.

The gears inside spun to life. With a low, ancient groan, the great door began to open, slowly at first, then fully flooding the chamber with golden light. And waiting on the other side... was the ship.

Nestled within a massive underground cavern, it sat in still water at the edge of a stone dock, surrounded by softly glowing lanterns suspended like stars in the darkness. The cavern walls were sealed by blocks and stone, preserving the sacred history of this place for future generations, waiting to be uncovered by those willing to follow the clues.

If you seek, you find. And now, all the doors had opened.

The team stepped forward in silence, reverence in every footfall, awestruck by the sight before them. The ship was grand, ancient, yet remarkably preserved. Its three towering masts stretched into the shadows above, sails furled tight, and its dark, aged wood gleamed beneath the warm lantern light.

Every beam, every plank was shaped with craftsmanship and care, evidence of hands guided by wisdom and conviction. They climbed up and stepped onto the deck, their boots echoing softly on the polished wood. Puck looked up at the grand spreaders, resembling crosses that held the sails. He walked slowly to the rear mast in the aft area of the ship near the quarters. Inscribed in bold, enduring letters:

"The repentant lēstai."

Puck glanced back. "Care to provide the translation, Dr. E?"

"Greek," she replied, her voice reverent. "Often translated as rebels, bandits, or violent criminals, not ordinary petty thieves. The term used for the 'thieves' on the cross. Most scholars agree that it refers to insurrectionists. Those men were condemned for more than theft. They were most likely men of violence."

Puck moved to the next masthead in the center at midship and traced the inscription with his fingers:

"The King of the Jews."

Then, looking across the deck, he saw Zane standing near the forward mast.

"What's that one say?" he called out.

Zane glanced at the carved words.

"The unrepentant lēstai."

Puck paused, the weight of history pressing gently on his shoulders.

"One asked Jesus to remember him in His kingdom," he said quietly. "And the other... mocked Him."

"One repented," Tad added. "The other asked for a sign, for proof."

RaJohn stepped beside them, eyes steady. "That's what makes the difference, doesn't it? One had a change of heart... even in his final breath. The other clung to pride, demanding a miracle instead of surrendering."

He looked at the carved mast before him.

"Jesus said in John 3:18, 'He who believes in Him is not condemned, but he who does not believe is condemned already, because he has not believed in the name of the only begotten Son of God.'"

Puck nodded solemnly. "And Romans 3:10 reminds us, 'There is none righteous, no, not one.' No one earns it. Not one of us deserves it. But one of those men believed... and he was promised paradise."

The masts stood like eternal sentinels, choices carved in time. Two lives beside Christ. One heart softened. The other, hardened. Both saw the same Savior. One repented. One rejected. Truth preserved in wood and time.

The rest of the ship was quiet, clean, and shipshape. The team gathered in the captain's quarters. On the desk sat a well-worn Bible, a film case, and an old projector with a hand crank. A torn section of sailcloth hung on the wall beside it, with scriptures carefully stitched by hand. Behind the desk, rows of scrolls filled narrow wooden cubbies, each labeled with symbols, dates, and names.

Luna carefully loaded the film into the projector. Jones gave the crank a few firm turns, and to their surprise, the old machine came to life, projecting light and history across the far wall.

The film flickered on.

Black and white images filled the room of people working shoulder to shoulder. Hands building trains, crafting lighthouses, building ships, and shaping early aircraft. Engineers laying gears into the clock tower. Divers' testing suits. Families helping one another, praying, studying, and inventing. Teaching. Serving.

Then a voice began.

"Welcome, seekers and keepers of Truth, to our 'Tell.'
If you're seeing this, then you have traveled far. Not only in distance, but in heart, in teamwork, and in character.

You've uncovered a legacy not of secrecy... but of servanthood. We are a generation that believed that our talents, our design, our innovation, and our courage were meant to serve God and help others. We come from many places, many skills. But we were united by one Truth:
You are not here by chance.
You are wonderfully made in the image of God. You were designed with purpose and purchased with love."
The images shifted again, maps, globes, pieces of cloth with familiar symbols. Then footage of people building the very place they were in, placing the ship into its resting dock, locking the entrance, carving into beams, and etching symbols into the artifacts.
"We do not worship the earth. It is not our mother.
God is our Father.
That's the power of deception, it often imitates light, while hiding the Truth in plain sight.
Christ created all things. In Him, all things hold together. The Bible describes life in the blood, the changing seasons, and the creativity He passed on to us. As His image-bearers, we too design. We too build. And we are called to use these gifts for good."
The masts of the ship appeared next on screen.
"The three masts you saw above are more than structure; they are a testimony.
The King of the Jews stands in the center. On either side: two lēstai-rebels, insurrectionists, criminals.
One changed his heart and was promised paradise.
The other demanded proof. He refused to believe, even while dying beside the Truth Himself.
This is the choice every person must face."
Now the scroll cubbies, the map table, and the artifacts were shown, each placed with intention. "These symbols, the moon, gear, octopus, lens, they're not sacred.

They're signposts. They're reminders. They guide your eyes toward the One who is unseen. Like airmolcules that create lift in wings or thrust in sails, strong and unseen with the naked eye.

Moses asked God for His name... and was told, 'I AM that I AM.' Job was asked, 'Where were you when I laid the foundations of the earth?' He was reminded that even the Behemoth, tail like a cedar, was God's creation. Long before we ever mounted its bones in a museum, God had already described it in perfect detail. God does not change. And His Word remains."

The film returned to scenes of teamwork. Building. Serving. Planting.

"There are 'Tells' like this all over the world. Families pass them on. Some found their own, maybe even the same one you uncovered now. They might have been hidden in different ways, but always with the same heart: To pass on Truth. To build the next generation. To prepare the Church.

The Body of Christ isn't made of stone and stained glass. It's made of you. Each of you brings strengths, and in your weakness, you've already seen how His strength carries you. When you are connected to the Head, Christ, you know your purpose.

Serve His purpose. And lead others to Him."

Now, the video faded into a still image, three keys, three words: Time. Space. Matter.

"You now stand in the same place we once did. The next step is yours. Stay on the path. Expose the works of darkness. Plant seeds that will return a harvest.

Teach others. Leave behind your own trail of truth. You may choose to return these artifacts or hide them in new ways, new 'Tells,' that another generation will one day discover. You may also choose to create new artifacts, teach the world what you've learned.

152

The image on the wall shimmered in the quiet hum of the projector's final frames. Then the voice spoke once more, gentle, clear, and full of resolve:

"Before the light fades, there's one more truth to leave with you.

Out on the open sea, a ship can lose sight of the stars. Storms may cover the heavens, and darkness may hide the horizon. But the lesser lights, the moon that commands the tides, the compass needle points, the feel of the wind in your sails, can still guide you forward. These are not just tools. They are gifts, like wisdom passed from one generation to the next.

The rudder may be small, but it turns the ship. The wheel requires steady hands. And the sails...oh, the sails must be trimmed and ready to catch the breath of wind at just the right moment. The Scriptures say the Spirit moves like the wind; you don't know where it comes from or where it's going, but if your sail is up, you'll be carried along with great force.

The body of Christ is much the same. Every person, every skill, every moment of courage, every act of service is like rigging, timber, or canvas. Alone, they're only parts. But when joined together in faith and unity, they carry the Gospel forward across oceans of darkness.

Some of you will reset this 'Tell.' Some will build new ones. Some will leave behind clues, journals, maps, or a single symbol carved into stone. But all of you are now part of the legacy.

And remember: the journey is not about the tools, the artifacts, or even the ship. It's about the direction. It's about the Truth. You are not an accident. You were called. And though you may not always see the stars, stay on course.

May God fulfill His purpose in your lives and may all glory be to Him, forever."
The film clicked to a stop.

153

Silence settled over the cave. The golden lanterns flickered gently across the deck of the hidden ship, their light dancing on the faces of those who had chosen to answer the call. The Keepers stood together not as relic hunters or gear-wielding travelers but as a team, united in Truth.

But its message still echoed like a whisper on the water.
A new course lay ahead. And they were ready to sail.
They stepped back onto the deck, where Rose stood waiting beside Needle and Rudder.
"Pretty awesome stuff, isn't it?" Rose said with a warm smile.
Puck tilted his head. "Rose... you knew all along?"
"Well," she said, "this whole town was built on it. Our ancestors handed this 'Tell' down, generation to generation. So yes. They wanted artifacts, history, and legacy to be an adventure like our faith. This town has always valued history. And tomorrow, if you'll join us, it's Sunday. We'll be at church. You're all Keepers of the Faith. The town would love to meet you."
She motioned toward the dock. "Why don't you reset everything and meet me back at the inn. Come back the way you came from the library entrance. We'll have some hot tea and fresh pastries waiting." The team nodded. Quietly, with a new sense of reverence, they retraced their steps. Together, they packed the artifacts, reset each door, and restored the 'Tell' to its sacred stillness.
Each artifact could rest in its original place or perhaps find a new home, like the gear, and they could make a new map for the octopus bottle. A future team might stumble upon this same story... or begin one of their own. And like the 'Tells' passed from one generation to the next, the Truth was buried and rose again. It was history that tells of Truth, and now, the Keepers carried Truth with them.

They returned through the library passage and emerged once more into the warm stillness of the inn. The fireplace glowed softly. Rose had already stoked the coals, as if she knew they'd be back soon. Needle curled up beside her chair, while Rudder rested faithfully at her feet, eyes half-closed but always watching.

The team gathered around the hearth with mugs of hot tea and plates of warm pastries. The firelight danced on the walls, casting long, shifting shadows. Each one is unique, yet drawn together by the same flame.

They didn't speak much.

They didn't have to.

They were all busy minds, going over everything they had just encountered. The journey hadn't just uncovered lost artifacts, secret chambers, or buried history. It had uncovered Truth, revealing deeper revelations, and it only scratched the surface. That night, they turned in with full stomachs and quiet minds, sleeping deeply, wrapped in peace. And when morning came, the scent of fresh coffee and homemade toast pulled them from slumber like the promise of a new day.

After breakfast, they helped Rose tidy up, an unspoken thank you for all she'd done. Then, stepping into the golden light of the Port of Valor, they strolled the cobblestone streets together. This time, they saw the town not as a mystery, but as a sanctuary. Every weathered stone and timber beam held a story.

At the church, Rose introduced them all before the service began. Pastor Richard welcomed them with warmth and gratitude, recognizing in these young faces the answer to years of quiet prayers.

The message that morning was simple and timeless:

Follow the Light. Serve others. Forgive as God has forgiven you. Work as the Body of Christ. Follow Christ's Gospel. Love.

And they knew in their hearts, they had grown in the last day.

They were part of the Body. A family.
Keepers of a calling that would never grow old.
When the time came to say their goodbyes, they returned to the inn one last time.
They knelt to hug Needle and Rudder, grateful for the quiet companionship and unwavering loyalty the animals had offered throughout the night.
A gift of thanks was left on the kitchen table for Rose.
She shook her head gently. "Family doesn't pay to stay. You helped Elias, and that's more than enough."
But Luna smiled. "A worker is worth their wage."
Rose's eyes misted as she accepted it. "Then I'll take it and bless someone else with it someday."
Outside, the sea breeze welcomed them home.
The morning sun shimmered across the surface of the harbor, and the sails of truth still caught the invisible wind.
The compass pointed north. The course was steady.
They had found the path.
By the lesser lights, the moon and stars, they would continue to navigate it.
The moon, ever faithful in its dance with the tides, reminded them that even in darkness, light remains.
The compass, like the Word, pointed them towards home, unmoved by shifting seas around them.

The rudder, small but mighty, steered their course with precision, directed by the hands of faith.
And the sails, like the Spirit, caught the wind unseen, moving them forward with power and grace.
For those who had eyes to see, these weren't just tools of navigation; they were signs and symbols of a greater journey.
The Tale of the Tells wasn't over. It had only just begun.
The Keepers would always have the Gospel to tell others. We all start off as one of the lēstai. Truth sets us free.

On the journey home, the team synced up with the Vaultrium and hailed Dr. E, Celeste, and Shonté to debrief. The connection was steady, the screen split with two friendly faces. Each of them smiled to see the team after their adventure.

"You all look like you've been dragged through sand and saltwater," Dr. E teased.

"Pretty accurate," Zane replied with a tired grin. "Except it was more relic dust and tunnel muck."

Agent Hardee, flanked by a digital map with scrolling data entered the chat.

The team perked up. They hadn't heard from Hardee or the other half of the operation in nearly two days.

Puck, riding his motorcycle alongside Tad and Zane, grinned. "Well, if it isn't the shadow side of the mission."

Hardee smirked. "You know us, just pushing paper and pulling threads. But good news: we've made solid progress with several branches of the government. They're finally starting to connect the dots."

The mood in the transport lightened.

Hardee continued, "Since Senator Slate and the Vale cousins were exposed, security efforts went full swing with intel gathering, inter-agency cooperation, and locking down gaps. Slate's being formally charged, and we've got active warrants on the Vale boys. So far, we've hit three of Jonah's target locations. Empty. Cleaned out before we arrived. They've gone to offshore, underground, or underwater."

He paused, his tone growing heavier. "But make no mistake. RIPTIDE crossed a line. They hit civilians. Homeland. That triggered something that has struck a nerve. We're finally being listened to. Senator Johnson and Wes are pushing for more action." "Good," said Luna from the command truck. "Now maybe we can start getting somewhere."

Hardee nodded. "That's the plan. Oh, and we watched some of the feed from the Port of Valor op. Epic stuff. What you all pulled off was clean, daring, and strategic. Jonah even replayed a few angles to admire the views."

Puck smiled. "It was... educational. And an adventure."

He leaned forward on his bike. "Say, you wouldn't happen to know anything about these 'Tells'... would you?"

Hardee chuckled. "Figured it out, did ya? Becker and I had our own run with that kind of mission. But this one was yours. There are a few others out there - some known, some forgotten, some still being built. You never really know when you'll find one... or create one. Not until the moment's right."

The comms quieted for a moment.

Then - a soft vibration.

Zane glanced down. "Uh... is anyone else's cube..."

A low, resonant pulse came from the cubes in their belts. Each team member's cube glowed faintly and pulsed in synchronized rhythm. It wasn't intense, just noticeable.

Luna tapped hers. "They're... resonating. Same frequency."

Celeste looked offscreen, checking a nearby console. "Dr. E?"

Dr. E was already examining readings, eyes narrowing. "It's the lost cube. The one RIPTIDE took."

Everyone froze.

"The signal is faint," she continued. "But it's active - and that means they're trying something,"

Becker's voice suddenly cut in over the line, voice full of amused defeat. "Well... I guess I blew the surprise."

The team laughed. Puck leaned forward. "Becker?"

"Hey, family," he said with a grin. "Glad you're all safe. We'll talk more when you get home."

"Wait," Tad said, "you're already back at the Forge?"

"Yep. Took a little time after being rescued to be with my wife... but I couldn't stay away. Can't wait to see you."

As the transport rolled deeper into the quiet hills, each member took time to make brief, private calls home. Updates were shared. Jokes exchanged. Just enough normal to remind them of why they did what they did. They decided it was time to plan a visit for families to join them for a tour of the Forge in the near future. As the team convoy rolled up to the gates hidden like a maze in the natural surroundings, they could almost taste the sense of home just beyond the bend. Team TIDES pulled in and parked their vehicles safely inside the facility. Becker, Dr. E, Celste, and Shonté were standing around, proud and ready to share the evening with them. They dropped their gear, cleaned up quickly, and settled in around the long table. The meal was casual and communal. Conversation flowed easily, like family after a long time apart.

Later that night, the team gathered again. This time suited up in full Frogman Mode. Sleek suits shimmered under the moonlight as they walked to Frogman Bay.

RaJohn helped Shonté board one of the octopods, and the two glided under the surface, dipping beneath in silence.

Dr. E and Celeste trailed behind in a second pod.

Becker stepped beside Puck. "You ready?" Puck smiled. "Always." The Frogman team dove in silent and fluid.

The suits responded instantly, nanobot-assisted propulsion launching them through the freshwater tunnels, seamlessly adapting to pressure, direction, and motion.

Light strips embedded in the tunnels activated as they passed, illuminating crystal walls, embedded tech veins, and intersections leading to deeper chambers, some freshwater, some brackish, some opening toward the ocean.

No mission tonight. Just rhythm. Motion. Bond.

As the team swam, Puck caught the reflection of Luna's cube through the water. It pulsed faintly, just once. Then again.

He filed it away. Tomorrow would bring questions.

But tonight... the TIDES were aligned.

# The Heart of the Forge

At sunrise, the Forge was already humming with quiet energy. After a quick breakfast, the team filed into the Vaultrium. The walls pulsed faintly with cube light, soft hues casting long rays over the table where mission planning always began. Dr. E stood at the front with Celeste beside him, the large holo-map displaying global points of interest blinking red, others still gray.

"Now that we're back online," Dr. E began, "we need to distinguish between the two teams for field reports and operations." Luna raised an eyebrow. "We're going official?" "It's time," said Becker, stepping in from the rear, arms crossed with his usual wry grin. "You're a growing pod. Might as well wear the name with purpose." After a few suggestions, laughs, and honest thoughts, they agreed:

Puck's team would be called Tidecore, the central wave of field-ready frogmen and cube operatives based at the Forge.

Hardee's team would carry the name Tidelink, honoring their wide-range missions across governments and linking alliances.

"Good," said Hardee, patched in via comms. "Now that the names are set, let's talk real threats. Overnight, we got a pulse reading from the cube network. Dr. E, care to brief the team?" Dr. E nodded and brought the map back into focus. Signal threads snaked across the globe, converging in small clusters. "Here we have Tidecore," she said, highlighting their current location. "And here, Tidelink. But here... and here..." She tapped two more locations. A subtle static ripple passed through the table surface as a faint red glow lit the areas. "We've got another set of pings. Not from our network.

"Not from any known allied source," Dr. E repeated, voice low. "The signature is similar to ours - but altered. Inverted."

The room fell silent.

"That can only mean one thing," she said. "They've had some success making their cube parasitic... destructive... harmful. Like a leech sucking the life out of something good. More of them are showing up - and that's why we're getting notified."

Hardee's voice came through the comms again, grim. "Since Dr. E shared her intel with us, we've been able to tap into deeper systems with help from new allies. And we found this."

The Halo Hub flickered, and the holo-map shifted to high-resolution satellite imagery. The photo zoomed in on a shipping yard along the docks. It was unmistakable: Desmond and Corbin Vale, suiting up in dark, angular Anti-Frogman gear, standing beside a shadowy trench coat figure. Nearby, Eclipse loomed, his gloves glowing faintly with residual charge. But one figure stood out: a man in a stained lab coat, large, round goggles, dirty gray hair, and an eerie calm in his expression.

"We all know the Vales," said Hardee. "And Eclipse needs no introduction. But that man... that's no neighborhood family doctor." Dr. E stepped forward, pulling up a file with a red warning seal across the top. "His name is Dr. Calder Marrick. Former geneticist. Lost his license over a decade ago after being exposed for illegal cross-species experimentation including wildlife and humans. They were all horrible disasters."

Puck's eyes narrowed. "He's the guy who tried to create 'hybrid enhancements' from animal DNA, right?" "Exactly," Celeste confirmed. "Tried to prove he could make humans faster, stronger... by rewriting what was never meant to be altered. The results were tragic. Fatal. Costly. He disappeared after being blacklisted and disavowed. Rumors say he shifted into mind control experiments - first animals, then people."

"And now," Becker said, voice grim, "he's working with RIPTIDE, that's just great."

"Now that we've confirmed three elite RIPTIDE operatives," Dr. E said, tapping the holomap, "we're assigning code names. Corbin Vale is now Undertorque. Desmond Vale will be Darkwake. And Dr. Marrick... well, we're calling him Dr. NeuroVex, or just Dr. Vex. Whichever floats your boat."

The team burst into laughter, the tension snapping like a rubber band. Tad leaned over, gasping between chuckles. "If it's not code names or Choppa-Choppas, it's code names for code names... and acronyms for super high-tech amphibious gear!" Austin jumped in, grinning widely. "I love this stuff! Real sneaky government codes and spy ops lingo? Keep it coming. It's like a dream come true!"

"Speaking of dreams coming true," Hardee cut in over the comms, "we now have access to new detainment facilities through the defense department. They can move targets by ground, air, or sea, no handoffs, no leaks. These holding sites are state-of-the-art, part of a secure branch called the ARC Network. Different sites are built for different classes of threats, so when we take down someone like Eclipse or Ironshade again, they'll have no way out." He continued, his tone sharpening. "Since these signatures are showing up on our radar, we're likely going to see more direct contact with RIPTIDE soon. We'll map out the pings and move in as soon as we spot a pattern. We can't wait too long. If they replicate too many of those parasitic cubes, we'll be outnumbered." Hardee's voice grew heavier. "The good news is Dr. E built this tracking feature into the prototype. The original cube was Slate and the Vale brothers' play from the start... or should I say Undertorque and Darkwake."

The team shared a quick chuckle before Hardee pressed on. "We've traced the mess back to our early progress checks with partners tied to Slate's office. Becker was supposed to meet them when he was overrun and taken hostage. They didn't like how fast we were moving and decided to blindside us, steal our

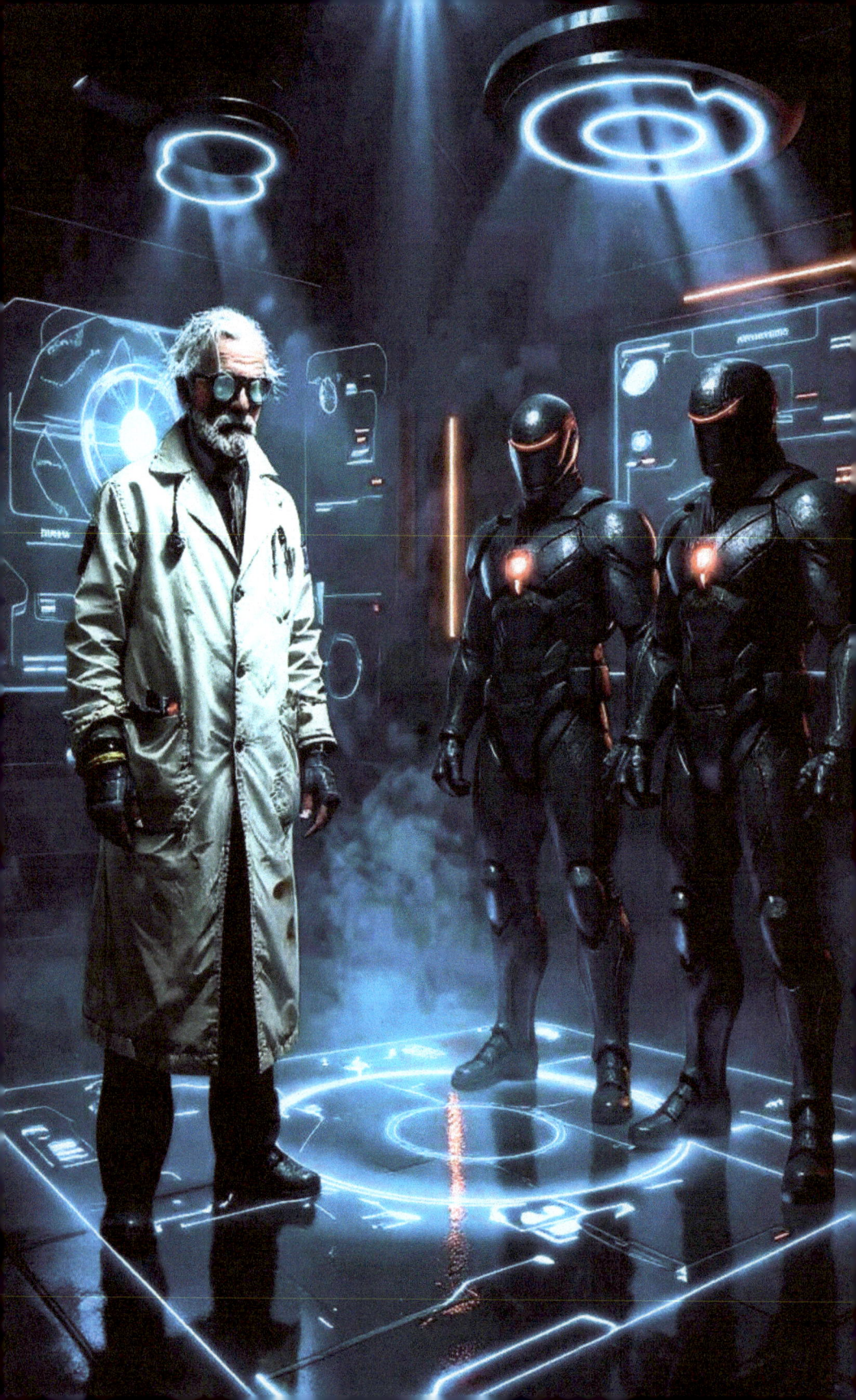

tech before we knew what hit us. Hardee's voice softened. "That's enough business for now. Tidelink's packing up and heading your way. We'll be at the Forge before the day's out, so get ready because we're bringing the families in, all of them."

Dr. E stepped forward beside the holo-map, holding a case of sleek Tide bands. "Ride-Along Mode is now active in your bands. Sync your loved ones to you, keep them safe, and let them experience what we do without risk. You'll see why I've been working on this feature soon enough."

In minutes, the holo-map shifted from red pings to glowing markers, not targets, but homes. Routes lit up like threads on a web. Both teams fell into an instinctive rhythm, plotting pickups and sequencing arrivals like a mission. Tidecore began fanning out across their territory, while Tidelink coordinated their sweep from Hardee's location, syncing each family's journey to converge at the Forge.

By midday, the base felt alive in a way it hadn't in months. Parents, siblings, and spouses stepped through the main access bays, wide-eyed as they entered the heart of Team TIDES' world. And when Tidelink finally arrived, the celebration swelled.

The tour wound through Frogman Bay, where octopods gleamed in their berths, then into the Synchronium, transformed into a sunlit beach with warm sand, volleyball nets, and a holographic ocean stretching beyond the horizon. Octopod rides, hoverboard races, and short flights above the shoreline filled the afternoon. In Frogman Mode, some families dove into the clear water alongside their Tide band partners; others soared high in Flight Mode, looping lazy arcs in the bright sky.

Then, after a full day of adventure, they all aligned in the Vaultrium, and Dr. E unveiled her newest creation, the DRIFT Droid.

At first glance, it appeared to be an art piece more than a machine. Its surface shimmered like a living nautilus, light rippling softly across its curved shell. As she activated it, the droid stirred, rising silently on a cushion of pale blue plasma. "Meet the Dynamic Response Intelligent Field Technician, DRIFT Droid," she said, pride glowing in her eyes. "Designed to protect, assist, and connect every one of you, wherever you are."

Everyone leaned forward as the droids rose. One moment, a cuttlefish, then and octopus, a jellyfish; the next, a stingray unfurling its wings. When Dr. E tapped her wristband, the droid spiraled upward, projecting a translucent holo-shield that rippled outward and down around her. "This field can deflect debris or deliver non-lethal deterrents if something breaches your perimeter," she explained. "Think of it as your silent guardian."

Gasps spread through the crowd as the droid separated into small nanobots that zipped through the air, reforming as one with a flash. "Adaptive defense and exploration. It can scout ahead, map terrain, even slip under barriers in nanobot form." Her tone softened as she guided the droid closer to the families. "It's a safety measure for your protection, and we are finalizing protocols for use within Team TIDES as a mission operative for each team member."

The droid descended again, folding into a delicate seashell, settling on her hand. "When dormant," Dr. E continued, "it draws almost no power. But when activated, it links with your Tide Band to extend its range and sync your environment to the same protection network that guards our operations."

Her voice grew thoughtful, almost reverent. "In time, each DRIFT unit will be part of the Vaultrium relay. Just like the team's suits, it is charged by solar power, and they quickly adapt to threats in real-time."

Compact and versatile, it could deploy into patrol, guardian, or comm relay modes in seconds. "It's not a spy," she said with a grin, "but if danger ever comes to you, it will be your eyes, shield, and voice to Team TIDES." Dr. E handed each family a DRIFT Droid shell.

Meals were shared in the dining hall, long tables lined with seafood, fresh bread, and laughter. The full team, Tidecore and Tidelink together, gathered with their families around the fire pits on the Forge's outer decks, telling stories until the stars were high.

For a few precious hours, no one was a soldier or operative. They were just people, bound by faith, love, and the knowledge that whatever came next, they would not face it alone. The family was brought into the fullness of everything they were accomplishing, and with every step of faith out into the world, with darkness came risk. Team TIDES had already seen that RIPTIDE was not holding back on vulnerable soft targets, and it was time to step up one place higher to be ready if anything happened on the home front. They only way to stay ahead of the opposition, was to plan to be ahead.

The final part of the day was taking the families into the Synchronium to teach them how to use their DRIFT droids. The warm beach projection glowed under soft twilight lighting as operatives demonstrated each mode, guardian, comm relay, patrol, while loved ones practiced activating them, syncing them to their Tide Bands, and running basic commands.

When the lessons were done, the mood softened again. Some family members said their goodbyes, slipping away for the night. Other responsibilities were waiting back home. Others decided to stay in the Forge's guest quarters, eager to spend more time in the safety of the base and soak in the rare chance to be part of this world.

By the time the last round of desserts and coffee was served, the decks were quiet and the night settled in.

# In the Watch of the Night

The wind blew softly, and the base's lights dimmed to night mode. Tidecore and Tidelink lingered together a little longer, whispering around the embers in the fire pits before drifting to their quarters.

They did not know the peace would not last.

In the deepest hours of the night, the Forge's alert tone cut through the silence. The sharp, pulsing signal pulled every operative to their feet. Doors slid open, boots hit the floor, and comm channels came alive with Hardee's voice.

"Team TIDES, we have simultaneous activity. Tidecore, you are heading east. Tidelink, you are with me in the north sector. Details in the Vaultrium in two minutes."

No one hesitated. Gear was on, cubes synced, and they were ready for whatever waited in the dark; they would answer the call to action.

The team converged in the Vaultrium. All eyes locked on the holographic display as Dr. E pointed to two glowing clusters on the map.

"Team, we have two separate signals," she said. "One here in the north at the factory district, and one here in the east at the docks. Both locations show several active RIPTIDE operatives on thermals."

Puck leaned forward. "We know they have active cubes, but we still do not know what they are doing. Maybe it is time for some covert recon to see exactly what we are up against."

"That is exactly what I am thinking," RaJohn replied.

"Perfect," Hardee said. "Get in, find out what they are doing, gather as much intel as you can, and we will go from there."

Both teams engaged Flight Mode. Their systems locked onto potential threats and probable insertion points. The night air filled with the soft hum of propulsion as they rose above the trees and swept east and north toward their targets.

Tidecore reached the docks in the east first. It was a vast shipping and receiving yard, stacked high with containers and flanked by massive freighters moored along the piers. The harbor lights washed the steel maze in a pale orange glow, their reflection rippling across the black water. Puck, Tad, and Becker dropped lower, slipping silently into the water in Frogman Mode. Their suits adjusted to the water instantly, seals locking tight as they submerged and glided toward a rust-streaked freighter from the harbor side. At Becker's hand signal, they engaged RGM. Without a sound, they scaled the freighter's hull until each had reached an observation perch.

James, Zane, and RaJohn moved higher, securing position atop a towering crane that overlooked Dock B. RaJohn's voice came over the secure channel, low and steady.
"Overwatch, top of crane on Dock B. Eyes on."

Luna and Jones made a rooftop landing on a warehouse at the far end of the pier, staying low as they crawled forward to get a harbor-side view. Through their optics, the scene came into focus.

Four RIPTIDE agents stood in loose formation near a stack of black shipping crates. Beside them were men in long, dark trench coats, their faces hidden in shadow. Another pair, instantly recognizable as Darkwake and Eclipse, paused for a moment like they were waiting for something. Then, one of the agents brought over a crate and slowly opened it. Inside, cubes pulsed with a deep, blood-red glow; their light was sharp. Eclipse gestured toward the cubes as one of the trench coat figures leaned in, clearly intrigued. It was a demonstration, the kind meant to sell power to the highest bidder. Each Tidecore operative tagged an individual target in their HUD, activating directional microphones to isolate the conversations.

Then, a new overlay appeared on everyone's display: two icons, one of a bat and the other of a dolphin.

Dr. E's voice came over the comm.

"I've got local wildlife in range. Symbiotic cubes are now linking to their echolocation streams. Bats will provide close-quarters mapping of containers and structures. Dolphins will give you a complete three-dimensional overlay of the underwater world, from the harbor floor to every submerged structure within range."

The HUDs shifted instantly.

The bat feed traced rapid, high-frequency sweeps through the maze of containers, painting sharp silhouettes of hidden movement. Figures were slipping between stacks, a pair of armed guards tucked in shadow.

The dolphin feed rolled in next, deep clicks translating into a living sonar map of the harbor's depths. The visualization revealed schools of fish, anchor chains stretching into the dark, and the skeletal frame of a half-sunken barge. But one signal stood out, moving steadily beneath the freighter.

"Submersible contact, starboard side, moving fast," Puck murmured. He pivoted from his position to underwater and launched a micro-GPS tracker from his gauntlet. It struck the shadow cleanly.

From their vantage points, James and RaJohn watched as one of the trench coat figures produced a portable console, linking directly to one of the parasitic cubes. The red glow intensified as a nearby crane shuddered, the cube draining power straight from the dock's systems. Lines of data spilled through the open airlink. "Dr. E, are we catching this?" Becker asked quietly. "Affirmative," she replied. "Every time they activate in leech mode, the original firmware still pings our network. It's not just biotech; it can also target infrastructures. Trackers are showing some activity, but not consistently. Must be the cubes.

They don't know they're giving us a location stamp with cube activity. If we can't always rely on trackers, at least we have that."

Eclipse gestured toward a nearby cargo truck, and they began loading crates into the trailer.

Becker keyed the channel. "Any container or truck that leaves, tag it anyway."

Puck's tone sharpened. "And we find out where they're manufacturing these cubes and take them down."

In the harbor, the dolphins' sonar feed showed the tagged submersible slipping away beneath the freighter, heading toward deeper waters. Another breadcrumb. Another lead.

RaJohn's visor caught Darkwake leaning in close to one of the buyers. Through the directional mic, his voice came faint but clear.

"The bidding has started. This isn't some endless market. You come in high, or you go home with nothing. And if your rivals get this tech before you..." He let the sentence hang, the unspoken threat heavier than the night air.

Eclipse stepped forward, resting one gloved hand on the open crate. The pulsing red glow of the parasitic cubes washed over his face like a mirror of burning light.

"This is the real deal," he said evenly. "You win tonight; you win forever. You lose, and you'll be owned by whoever does."

One of the buyers shifted uncomfortably but nodded. Another smirked, already calculating. No one here doubted that owning these cubes meant power, absolute control.

Above, RaJohn kept his gaze locked on Darkwake.

"Time is ticking," the RIPTIDE operative said into his buyer's ear. "Be there with your best offer. There's no second chance. No negotiation."

Eclipse and Darkwake packed up and left, heading north.

Tidelink reached the warehouse in silence, each operative moving into position with the precision of a clockwork mechanism. The building sat in the heart of the industrial district, its brickwork scarred by decades of hard labor and harder deals. Sodium streetlamps flickered overhead, washing the cracked pavement in a sickly amber haze.

They spread out. Some took the high rooftops of a neighboring factory; others pressed into shadows along the fireescapes.

Their dynamic camouflage blended so perfectly that if an onlooker thought they'd seen movement, they would blink and convince themselves it had been nothing more than the wind playing tricks.

Hardee's voice was a whisper over comms. "Eyes sharp. We are here to watch, not to be seen."

From his perch, Jonah shifted his optics until the image sharpened. Four RIPTIDE operatives were in view, standing in a loose semicircle. Facing them were three men cut from another era. The towering men were dressed in entirely pinstriped suits with the cut of old-world tailoring, shoes polished to mirrors, hands heavy with rings. The leader stepped forward, a broad man with a face like weathered stone. A cigar smoldered, smoke curling lazily around the brim of his fedora.

"That's him," Jonah murmured. "Vincent 'Stoggs' Marreti. Old-school mob, dockside roots, built his empire one bribe and a broken jaw at a time."

Stoggs took a long stare at the RIPTIDE agents, his voice a gravelled rumble that carried even at this distance. "You boys say this tech of yours changes the game. I'm listenin'. But I don't buy fairy tales, so make me believe it. Where are they? I don't like waiting." The tone was pure old mob boss. He was slow and deliberate, with the weight of a man who never needed to shout to get his way. "We have what you need to see tonight," answered the RIPTIDE agent.

Beside him, another man with a lean frame stayed half in shadow, eyes sharp as a knife's edge. The third man adjusted his tie and said nothing, his stare unblinking.

One of the RIPTIDE agents cracked open a heavy case, the lid hissing like it was alive. Inside, the crimson cubes pulsed. The glow spilled across the crates and the men's faces, staining them in shifting crimson.

Hardee's voice came low. "Tidelink, record everything. This is the same batch Tidecore intercepted. The bidding war just moved to the next stage."

Stoggs stepped closer to the cubes, the cigar's tip flaring as he spoke. "Looks pretty. But I don't pay for pretty. Show me what it does to an enemy."

The RIPTIDE handler smiled without warmth. "You'll see. But this is all or nothing. You want it, you bring more than your rivals. There is no second round."

Derrick muttered under his breath. "Classic play. Get them to overcommit and lock them in." Hardee's reply was sharp but quiet. "And we will find out where they are locking it in."

Beneath the murmur of mob voices, the cubes' low hum seemed to throb in the air, as if already feeding on the building's electricity. Somewhere behind the walls, a generator hiccupped, lights flickering before returning to life.

Jonah took aim and launched trackers, tagging each crate in view. "If those leave here, we can follow." One of the RIPTIDE agents set a cube on the warehouse's electrical box, connected it to a laptop, and turned the feed toward Stoggs. The lights around the warehouse faded as the cube went to work, drawing power and bleeding into the warehouse's network control systems.

In the half-light, Stoggs smiled, the kind of smile that promised nothing good. He gave a nod and pulled gently on the front brim of his hat.

The mob bosses turned without a word, stepping into dark sedans with tinted glass. Engines growled to life, tires spitting gravel as the convoy pulled away into the night.

One of the RIPTIDE agents raised his phone. "Boss, they're gone. Looked impressed. They'll come in strong, we've got them."

Dr. E's voice cut in over Tidelink's comms. "Heads up. Trackers from the harbor are pinging inbound. You've got company."

Within seconds, a pair of SUVs rolled up to the warehouse. Darkwake and Eclipse stepped out with a few RIPTIDE operatives. Their boots crunched against the cracked concrete as they moved towards the men already on site.

Darkwake's voice sounded digitized through his face shield, "*~Any sign they suspect the double-cross~?*"

"None," replied the RIPTIDE agent. "They think they're about to own the future. We'll let them play with the toys, get their little taste of power and profit, while the cubes drain their systems dry. Best part, we skim the cream off their own assets while they do the heavy lifting."

Eclipse's laugh was low and sharp. "When the order's complete, we take them down along with anyone else in our way. All the cores stay linked to HQ. They never really own a thing."

Austin's voice came quietly over comms. "I'm all for crazy covert ops, but this is next level. You've got RIPTIDE agents, mob bosses, and mystery trench coats planning a global takeover while RIPTIDE is leeching everyone, including the so-called allies. That's tense."

Darkwake turned to Eclipse. "*~The sub from the harbor will dock at the coastal site before sunrise. That decommissioned Naval base is key. High noon tomorrow, we start loading. We serve them back-to-back. After that... full distribution.~*"

Hardee's voice was calm but tight in Tidelink's ears. "Coastal site. That's HQ." Jonah added, "Figures. That old naval station

...was never fully decommissioned. That means the paperwork was just for show." Hardee didn't miss a beat. "We stage early. Noon, we cut this off before it leaves the ground or the water." From their hidden perches, Tidelink watched the last of the men disappear inside. The cubes' faint red glow still bled through the gaps in the crate lids, pulsing like a heartbeat. Tonight was recon. Tomorrow would be the biggest takedown yet. "That's it, team," Hardee said quietly. "We have what we need. Head home, get what rest you can. Align at the Vaultrium. Get some rest. We get to the old naval station before noon."

The purpose moved through them like a living current, syncing every operative in thought and movement. Their HUDs shifted to the optimal navigation route home as their suits transformed into Flight Mode. The moon hung full above the coastline, silver light rippling across the dark water as Tidecore lifted away from the docks. They knew they were meant to reflect God's light, pushing back the shadows and exposing the works of darkness.

From higher above the city, Tidelink passed over quiet neighborhoods, the warm glow of porch lights and streetlamps scattering across the streets. They were fighting for all of it, for the people sleeping peacefully below, for those who would never know the danger that pressed so close, even for those who stood on the wrong side. Everyone was at risk, whether they realized it or not. Little did the people in their cozy beds know how much effort was being spent to protect their freedom to choose, right or wrong, without the weight of control pressing on them. In perfect Sync Mode, the team prayed aloud: "God, give us the strength to do Your will. To fight the darkness and expose their ways. Amen."

One by one, they touched down at the Forge, retracting and powering down their suits. All of Team TIDES—Tidecore and Tidelink together—were back under one roof, ready to face the most intense mission since their alliance began.

# Clash of the Currents: The Symbiotic Stand

The morning came quickly, and the team had no time to lose. They rose, gathered for breakfast, and prayed for safety. Once the last plates were cleared, they headed straight for the Halo Hub in the Vaultrium.

Dr. E stood at the main holographic console, the aerial imagery of the old naval base spinning slowly in midair. "Here's the target. Officially decommissioned years ago... but it seems Senator Slate's connections paid off. They took the decommissioning funds, poured them into upgrades, and then quietly transferred the infrastructure to Shell Tech."

The map shifted to a layered overlay. "These scans show the original layout. This," she said, tapping a control, "is the new construction. Notice the large holding tank here, likely for Dr. Vex's twisted experiments."

Puck leaned in. "What kind of experiments?"

Dr. E's expression tightened. "From his history, I'd say mind-control trials... and an attempt to integrate the parasitic cubes into living hosts. Possibly marine life."

Lines on the map lit up in red, tracing from the shoreline out into the bay. "These conduits run beneath the water to what we believe is an underwater facility. No time for deep research before deployment. You'll have to launch underwater drones for a live map once you arrive."

She zoomed in on the docks. "This sector is their shipping and receiving hub for submersibles. Expect to see old pilings, rusted I-beams, and the skeletal remains of original structures, and a coms tower here. It's going to look like a wasteland... but those features will give you vantage points."

Another set of lines highlighted in gold. "We also believe this facility was never fully decommissioned. Paperwork was for show. That means older access points might still exist; let's use them."

183

The base layout shifted again, replaced by a rendered simulation. "James has loaded this into the Synchronium for a quick run. Get a feel for the terrain before boots hit the ground."

She gave them all a final look. "Choppa-Choppa, head over there now. And team... be safe."

They answered with tight nods and headed to the Synchronium to run their drills. The real thing was only hours away.

Team TIDES synced up, suits scanning the rendered simulation of the old naval base. In an instant, the terrain had unfolded beneath them. They launched over the layout, practicing suit transitions mid-flight, diving through choke points, and marking high-ground positions. Every turn and blind corner was etched into memory.

Minutes later, they gathered near the control console for a final rundown.

Agent Hardee faced them. "Let's talk tactics. What do you see based on the layout?"

Puck spoke first. "If all their operatives are present, and I'm betting they will be. Shatterborne will have to hold high ground, away from the underwater facility. Shatterborne's seismic hits and Eclipse's toxic EMP bursts would wreck their own infrastructure if they were too close, but someone's going to be with Dr. Vex, which is worrisome."

He pointed toward a high ridge on the hologram. "I'd place them here, well clear of the bay. However, they are reckless."

RaJohn nodded. "Terrablight will stick to dense foliage. He needs biomass for fuel. This sector's the best match. Ironshade's trickier; he could be anywhere."

"Anywhere," Hardee agreed, "as long as he's not inside the underwater base when he loses control. Be ready for rapid underwater extractions if he or Eclipse is down there. RIPTIDE doesn't mind sacrificing others or their own."

The team's expressions hardened in unison.

Hardee's voice was calm but firm. "I'm sending word to our full network of allies. We go in first, assess quickly, and keep backup on standby. Secure transport for elite RIPTIDE agents is a top priority. This mission is ours, but when the fight hits its peak, we will take every hand willing to stand with us. Is everyone ready?"

No one spoke, but in full sync, all visors in flight mode locked, and the destination dial in their HUD's showed Hardee that they were. Outside the Synchronium, the Forge crew and family members were already waiting in the morning light. The air carried the crisp scent of the coast, and gulls called faintly in the distance. They formed a circle around the team and prayed aloud for safety, victory, and a safe return. The final word was "Amen." Then the group stepped apart to let Team TIDES move out.

The sun was climbing, painting the rooftops in gold as the two units stepped outside in full gear. Without hesitation, they lifted from the ground, cutting through the clear morning air in tight formation. The ocean glittered below, sunlight rippling across the surface. In-flight, they confirmed assignments. Hardee, Derrick, Jordan, Austin, Jonah, Brox, and Ryan would take the high ground and Overwatch positions. Becker, Puck, Tad, Zane, Jones, James, RaJohn, and Luna would split between the entrance to the underwater base, the submersible port, and perimeter security. Every position came together like clockwork, each role reinforcing the others. Luna's voice broke the radio silence. "So, I'm back in Overwatch again? What, you think I can't keep up with the big guys?" Becker's voice came back with a grin in it. "You'll tag more RIPTIDE agents than the rest of us combined. We're just making sure you've got the angle to do it." Luna chuckled. "Fine. At least I won't have to give my David and Goliath speech again."

185

The laughter was short, but enough to cut the edge of tension. Hardee's voice came over comms, steady and commanding. "Multiple assets are in position and ready to move on my call. Stay tight, watch each other, and keep your head on a swivel." Puck's voice carried the weight of the moment. "This is what we were made for. Stand for the Truth, expose the works of darkness, and hold the line, even when the currents clash and shadows press in."

The team's focus locked in as the base came into view. Adrenaline built, but each member kept it in check, staying in perfect sync.

Puck, Tad, and Zane hit the coastline first, shifting into Frogman Mode. They released underwater drone constructs, handing control over to Dr. E at the Vaultrium, then slipped into the harbor's shadowed waters. Scaling the south harbor wall in stealth mode, they took up silent perches.

Luna, James, and Jones flanked east, moving toward the north side and working south through an abandoned building with broken glass crunching faintly under their boots.

Becker, RaJohn, Brox, and Ryan headed into the woodlands, ascending a rusted communication tower for a sweeping view. Austin, Jordan, and Jonah landed on the far side of the harbor, weaving through derelict offices and collapsed structures until they reached a clear vantage of the underwater base's main entrance.

"Now it's a sit-and-wait game," Puck murmured.

"Dr. E, anything on heat signatures from satellite?" Becker asked.

"Nothing yet. I've got all your positions locked, but no movement," she replied.

Time stretched. The tension tightened. Doubt whispered. Had they chosen the wrong location? Missed a key piece of intel? Then the ground shook. Not the chaotic, jagged rumble of Shatterborne's attacks — this was mechanical.

Derrick's voice came low but urgent. "Movement. Northwest woods. Ground is... lifting."

Through the foliage, what had seemed like a harmless garden rose on a massive platform. Soil crumbled away, revealing thick steel beneath. A hidden elevator reached the surface, and the metal doors slid open with a hydraulic hiss.

Out stepped Shatterborne. Each heavy step cracked the dirt, sending thin fractures spiderwebbing outward. He didn't rush forward; he scanned the treeline like he could feel them through the roots beneath his boots.

Hardee's tone stayed steady. "First player's on the field. Let's observe and read the lineup."

Before they could track his next move, a heavy sea gate in the harbor rumbled open. Water surged inward, and shadows passed through the opening. Dr. E's voice cut in. "Dolphins, two large sharks are all rigged with cranial control units. Vex is using them for mind-control ops. We free them, or they're weapons against us. And...submersible from the docks breached and pinged GPS right behind them."

The submersible slid into its berth like a predator returning to a lair. The upper hatch swung open, and Ironshade emerged, plated armor gleaming in the sun. His visor swept the area in infrared, searching for movement. He glanced toward Shatterborne and raised a power fist in a silent show of force.

Terrablight was next, agile and twitch-fast, clambering from the submersible's hull up a rusting service ladder. His forearm intakes hissed as they drew in plants near the docks, the fuel for whatever toxic compound brewed in the backpack tanks slung across his spine.

Then, from the far pier, Undertorque and Darkwake appeared. Their suits thrummed with an unnatural hum, parasitic cube hybrids grafted into their chests, power lines tracing back into control nodes at the spine. The air seemed to buzz around them, a low-pressure warning that whatever they'd done with the

...cube tech blurred the line between machine, parasite, and willpower.

Jonah's voice tightened. "That's six confirmed. Still no sign of Dr. Vex."

As if on cue, the massive holding tank at the far end of the yard vented a plume of superheated mist. The reinforced hatch turned, locks releasing with a heavy clang.

Water poured out as the creature crept forward. A giant octopus, its size unnatural, each tentacle rippling with muscle and glinting with an embedded parasitic control node.

Puck whispered, "What is that... a Kraken?"

Tad muttered, "If it is, I don't even wanna know what Vex has been feeding it."

Hardee keyed the comms. "Eyes up. We've got the whole storm in play. Wait for my mark."

Dr. Vex emerged from a path beside the tank. He had a control module pulsing with red light from the embedded parasitic cubes. A matching cube glowed from the octopus's cranial rig, pulsing together at the same time.

Austin quipped, "Can someone call Dr. Christenson and ask if I can keep the Kraken once we free it?"

Puck shot back, "I'll ask him myself, if you can get those creatures free and we secure the shipments before RIPTIDE hands them off."

Hardee's tone sharpened. "We can do it. Pick your targets and move!"

The symbiotic HRAM surged through every suit. They didn't need pings, not now. The core sync was alive, and the bond was unshakable. The first strike was theirs. Huds displayed the best angles of attack in sync. Hardee gave the order, "Team TIDES strike." It was like lightning came from every angle. Their suits blazed with energy and willpower, fueled by divine purpose in the show of intelligent design. Everything collided in an instant.

Hardee's voice cut through the comms, steady but urgent. "Full network alert. Coast Guard, ARC, and Homeland Security are inbound for perimeter containment and transport. Nobody leaves unless we say so. This base is locked down."

Affirmatives came back in chorus. The symbiotic HRAM Core pulsed in every suit, locking to monitor the creatures with parasitic cube nodes. HUDs flashed green as drones spun outward, feeding live perimeter maps. TENDRILS flexed in idle loops, ready to snap into combat or medical assist in a heartbeat.

The harbor stretched out in steel and shadows, pilings like the bones of giants, relics from a time when warships moored here.

## HARBOR FRONT — PUCK, TAD, ZANE

They slipped below the surface, the noise of the world above dimming into the low hum of the deep. Drones cut ahead, beams of light slicing through the water.

Dr. E's calm voice came over comms.

"Three dolphins. Two great whites. All show cube rigs. Vital monitors are spiking. Move fast."

Tad veered toward the first dolphin. He reached for its harness, but the creature panicked, thrashing violently. His HUD flared yellow. Pulse too high. Oxygen saturation was too low. He locked on with a TENDRIL, stabilizing himself, and ripped at the clamps until they tore loose. The dolphin screeched in the water, then bolted for the open sea.

Zane tangled with a great white. He deployed an ink cloud to confuse it, then darted under its belly and attached two TENDRILS into its rig. The shark twisted and slammed him into a piling. Zane's HUD screamed red from the impact. His suit enriched his facemask rebreather with oxygen, giving him seconds to fight through the haze. He fired a microdart into the buckle, then another, until the rig split apart. The shark wrenched free and swam off, vitals slowly returning to normal.

192

Puck had almost no time to react before the second dolphin rammed into him, controlled by its cube. He spun, grappling its harness, his TENDRIL snapping into the rig's fasteners. The dolphin shook violently. At the last second, Tad joined him, doubling TENDRILS around the node, and together they ripped it free. The dolphin stopped thrashing, steadied, and hovered close, watching them.

The water trembled. Shadows blotted out the light.

A mass rose from the depths like a living island.

The Kraken.

Tentacles the size of subway cars lashed out. One seized Tad, another wrapped Zane. Puck's heart hammered. He fired two blasts of cuttlefish-mesmerizing and transitioned to full dynamic camouflage to disorient the beast, then drove grapple TENDRILS around its cranial rig. The fasteners shrieked under strain. He pulled until the metal screamed and snapped. The rig crashed into the harbor floor.

The Kraken stilled.

Tad and Zane fell free, coughing into comms. Puck drifted in front of one vast eye, no larger than an insect in its gaze. He placed his hand against the creature's scarred forehead. The HUD pulsed. The symbiotic core surged. The Kraken's iris shifted, bleeding from parasitic red back to a natural hue. The cube's rhythm joined the team's, one steady rhythm across man and beast.

Then, gently, the Kraken reached out. It caught the last rigged shark in its coils, brought it to Puck like an offering. Puck tore the cube free. The freed shark rolled away, then circled back, not fleeing, but choosing to stay, sensing the symbiotic pulse. The dolphin that had bolted earlier returned, nosing close, as if drawn by the sync. One by one, the freed animals formed around Team TIDES, not prisoners anymore, but allies.

"Hardee," Puck said quietly, his voice carrying a fierce edge. "We've got friends in the water now. Let's make it count."

Inside a gutted warehouse, James raised a lattice of hardened constructs. Jones set sticky traps with TENDRIL bands across the ground, angling them toward a fault-line crack. Luna steadied her breathing.

The giant appeared, armored in metal, steps like tectonic plates grinding. His voice was thunder.

"Fee-fi-fo-fum... I smell the fear of a little one."

Luna smirked, her voice sharp. "Good thing I didn't pack fear. Just fight."

She fired a glob of goo straight between his eyes. Shatterborne clawed at the mess, stumbling. Jones snapped the first snare; the giant tripped, slammed his fist into the ground, and a shockwave shattered the ground. Luna rolled clear, snapping another shot into his knee joint.

"Trap two!" James shouted.

The net launched, tangling him. The ground split beneath his feet. Half his bulk plunged into the fissure, arms straining against goo and TENDRIL binds. He bellowed in rage, but the more he fought, the deeper the pit swallowed him.

Pinned.

Luna strode forward, chest heaving, visor reflecting the hulking prisoner at her feet.

"Guess I got my Goliath moment after all."

Woods High Ground — Becker, Derrick, RaJohn, Brox, Ryan vs. Terrablight

The forest had streaks of chemical burn. Terrablight moved like a wraith, vents hissing, forearms spitting sludge that hissed on contact with wood.

"You'll choke on my work," he spat, firing a stream that carved rot into a trunk.

"Split him," Becker ordered. RaJohn vaulted into view, mocking him with a taunt. Terrablight lunged, blinded by anger.

Brox's TENDRIL lashed his legs, Derrick dropped from a grapple line, and shot goo into the pack's vents.

The toxin sprayed, but the wind turned.

It washed back over Terrablight. His vents clogged, alarms screamed, and corrosion spread across his back. He howled.

Becker's team hosed him with probiotic mist. The hissing slowed. TENDRIL restraints locked tight, vitals normal.

"Terrablight secure," RaJohn called.

Becker checked his HUD, then broke east. "I'm helping Luna's team."

Brox and Ryan peeled west toward the docks.

WEST FLANK — AUSTIN, JORDAN, JONAH VS. IRONSHADE

The brute tore from the command center like a warhead. IR optics burned red, scanning for prey.

Austin fired a volley of darts. They sparked harmlessly. Jonah threw up a wall construct. Ironshade plowed through, slamming Jonah into concrete.

Jordan lashed his arm with TENDRILS. Ironshade hauled him close, trying to crush him. Austin snapped a whip around the other wrist. They strained, dragging him step by step toward the pier's edge. Brox and Ryan arrived, each latching him with a TENDRIL, pulling with everything their suits had.

Ironshade roared. He was slowing, but not broken.

INTERCUT — HARDEE

From Overwatch, Hardee's voice was iron.

"Containment perimeter sealed. Nobody breaks through. Hold them. Watch your backs, team."

Every HUD pulsed with the core sync. The freed dolphins and sharks circled like guardians. The Kraken loomed at the breakwater, its tentacles casting shadows over the docks.

The Kraken positioned Puck in the center of its forehead and moved into action. Puck rode the Kraken like a storm-tamer. The beast moved with the smoothness of a deep current, tentacles coiling and uncoiling as it bore him up the breakwater. The creature's head rose from the water like an island, and Puck found a standing hold on its broad forehead while the team watched from the docks, water streaming off the beast in silver sheets.

The Kraken's bulk swung a tentacle and closed on Ironshade, who had been fighting his way along the pier and was breaking free of the team on the dock. The great arm seized the brute and held him with crushing patience, lifting him clear of the dock and pinning him against a piling that supported the wharf. Sparks flew where plated armor met pure steel.

Jones whooped over comms, laughing. "Okay, if Puck gets a Kraken to ride, I want an iron-horse construct to ride in battle." A few team members gave thumbs-up. The sound cut the tension for one thin breath.

The Kraken tilted Ironshade so that Jordan, steady on the dock, could aim at a seam in the shoulder plates. Jordan fired a tranquilizer that landed with surgical precision. The huge suit's servos eased. Jordan's HUD flashed; vitals stable.

Tad's voice was dry as salt. "Night-night, Ironshade. That's twice now. Remember, crime doesn't pay."

The Kraken set Ironshade into the dock in the waiting hands of Brox and Ryan. Puck slid off the beast's brow and stuck a smooth landing on the dock. He reached and brushed the Kraken's slick skin. The animal dipped its head and slipped back beneath the surface, close enough to watch like a guardian.

Hardee keyed a command. Task overlays bloomed on everyone's HUD. Modular carriers with lockdown straps and vitals monitors powered into position. The team built a chain to Hardee's holding teams, who were now waiting on standby.

Dr. Zayler chimed from the Vaultrium. "Heads up. Hardee's callout is en route. They will break through the south wall. You will see comms traffic on HUDs in ten seconds. Rose, Elias, and Pastor Richard are cutting in now. Shonté and Celeste are at the tunnel junction in an octopod for comm links handoff. They are in classic frogman gear but picking up some Forge tech for comms." Puck, Tad, Zane, and the Kraken slipped beneath the surface again to watch the arrival. Darkwake and Undertorque were somewhere out beyond the light.

A deep mechanical thrumming moved through the harbor. Rose's hydro-powered cutter surfaced like a tube of iron with articulated legs. Pastor Richard and Elias handled fine details, standing at consoles while Rose worked the controls.

"We thought old school might finish what the new school starts," Rose said. "We're cutting a clean tunnel, setting anchors, and making a transport corridor. Shonté, Celeste, thanks for the hand-off. Those comms are slick." Puck replied, "No doubt that you three have many tricks lying around. Glad to have you."

The cutter chewed an arch through the old seawall. Hot plasma edges burned and seal-welded. Walking anchors punched neat holes into the substrate. Actuators shoved pre-cut blocks into place. The machine's reverse rotor spun a cylindrical current that cleared debris into neat spirals and deposited fine sand. Brutal, precise, and beautiful.

Then the water dimmed. A black cloud spilled like ink across shafts of light. Undertorque and Darkwake burst the surface in twin arcs, suits humming with parasitic power, red cubes glowing in the center of their chests. They fired a dense black toxin that smeared the surface area of the water and swallowed daylight. The harbor went to a false midnight.

Dr. E flagged HUD protocols. "Night vision on. Switch all bands to low-light spectral feeds. Austin, detox field at your ready."

Austin grinned and launched from a hoverboard. "Time for a bio-clean run." He sprayed symbiotic probiotic mist in a wide arc. The droplets shimmered pearlescent. Where the mist kissed the toxin, it hissed and shrank. The surface began to clear as the mist neutralized the toxins.

The two enforcers moved like a sickness. Their parasitic hybrid cores reached out, leeching vitality from plants and fish. Green foliage dulled, schools slowed, and poisoned micro-darts clipped Puck, Tad, and Zane. Zane's reflex net shot out and caught a dart. The poison sizzled through the weave. A red beam lanced from Undertorque's gauntlet and nicked Puck's suit core. His HUD blinked small losses in stored power.

Puck's jaw set. He spoke, voice steady and as sharp as a double-edged sword. "No weapon formed against us shall prosper." The prototype symbiotic cube on his belt flared white. The Heart Core responded. It was fueled by Truth. The Living Word of God was alive. A pulse moved like a heartbeat through every suit. HRAM synchronized reflex matrices. Puck's cube emitted a strong, earthy prebiotic pulse that hit the water and every HUD. Where the pulse struck the black toxin, it smoked and burned to residue. Ionic detox fields flared. Plants brightened. Fish sped up. The harbor breathed again.

Symbiotic tools locked in. They exuded a frog-skin mucus shield, a shimmering biofilm that clung around their suits and sealed vulnerable joint seams against corrosive darts. Zane engaged the cuttlefish-mesmerizing and bent the light into liquid ripples, confusing his targets to make a strike. Puck and Tad's underwater drones released sonic burst fields as they chased down the anti-frogman. Cascades of ionic pulses danced through the water and severed node bonds on the parasitic rigs. Dolphins keyed into the Heart Core signal and sent precise sonar patterns that mapped Undertorque and Darkwake in three dimensions and guided team targeting.

Rose reversed the cutter's waterjet nozzles and built a vortex that caused focused turbulence around the anti-frogmen. Pastor Richard and Elias leaned out and fired a tethered trip line that snaked out and wrapped around Undertorque's leg and Darkwake's arm. The cutter's current spun them off balance. The Kraken rose and watched the tangled men slow to a halt. Its giant eyes were cathedral windows. A tentacle brushed each target as if to steady a child. Puck, Tad, and Zane surged as one. TENDRILS lashed, layered nets unfolded, microtranqs found seam joints, and Brox and Ryan dove to anchor the final lines. Within seconds, the enforcers were hogtied in layered restraints of securing bio-restraints.

Undertorque lashed with a last red draining beam. Puck braced as the Heart Core gleamed a bright white and emitted a visible shield of light around the team, blocking the red beam. His suit routed power to the TENDRIL launchers, which shot out of both gauntlets. They slammed into the chest mounts on Darkwake and Undertorque's parasitic cubes. Light surged down the TENDRILS in three pulses of power. The parasitic sync collapsed; the red glow faded to clear.

Rose killed the cutter's blades. It settled into the edge of the new underwater tunnel like a beast taking a bow. Pastor Richard and Elias swam down and slapped shoulders with Tad and Zane. Rose laughed. "Old school still gets the job done. But next time, we'll bring the nanobot watches. That was something else to behold." They swam to the surface as Rose continued, "The Word of God is alive, exactly like the book says." The Kraken folded and, careful as a parent, lifted the prisoners and set them on the dock where hovering transport pods waited. Carriers sealed with biofoam. Foam-based healing gel sloughed over abrasions. Stabilizers hummed. Ridge teams latched carriers and began the chain to the ARC Network.

Back at the surface, Jones assembled an iron-horse construct on the fly — a powered mount shaped like an armored stallion. He vaulted into the saddle and saluted.

"Iron-horse ready. Who wants a ride?"

Captives were loaded into transports. Jones guided the iron-horse up the ridge, escorting them toward the ARC hand-off team.

Rose and Puck stood at the pier's edge, watching the transports rise into the night sky. Below, the dark water rippled — Kraken waiting, patient as ever.

Puck spoke softly, not into comms: "Hold fast. We finish this together." Amid the movement and secured threats, Austin tapped Tad's arm.

"So... our tunneling cutter still needs a real name."

Tad nodded. "As long as it's not 'Choppa-Choppa.' We'll never hear the end of that."

Dr. E's voice chimed in, crisp:

"I can hear everything you say, gentlemen."

Austin cleared his throat quickly. "Right! Nominations. I'm saying Root-Cutter — because we cut corruption out by the roots!"

James hummed disapprovingly. "Sounds like a gardening tool."

Zane threw in, "Terra-Cutter. Simple. Tough."

Rose glanced at Luna — the grin between them said the boys are trying so hard. "We'll take all submissions under review," Rose said diplomatically. Dr. E added with a teasing edge:

"And we'll choose the name that doesn't sound like a weed-whacker." "Fair," Tad sighed.

Gear checks resumed.

Jones waved from the ridge as the iron-horse strode toward the ARC perimeter. Half the team remained to secure the site — the rest moved toward the deep, toward the shadows waiting below.

"Vex and Eclipse had to be down there. If Eclipse runs loose again, anyone below will face a bigger danger than they already know," Puck thought. Tidecore members RaJohn, James, Jones, Tad, Zane, Luna, and Puck headed to the entrance of the underwater base. Tidelink agreed to hold the docks and make their way underwater toward the submersible docking bay. The Kraken followed the submerging team closely.

They slid beneath the surface in pairs, suits sealing with a soft hiss. The water swallowed the noise of the world above, and focus narrowed to HUD readouts and the pulse of the Heart Core. Tidecore sent drones ahead for an interior scan of the base. A set of metal stairs descended through walls of solid rock, moisture dripping down the sides.

Light rigs on their drones painted the interior like searchlights through smoke. They located a level at the base of the stairs that opened into a large chamber, big enough for the tunnel cutter to enter. Rose, Elias, and Pastor Richard cut into the room at an upward angle, making room for a watery exit if needed. Mineral dust hung in slow motes after they cut through. The first drones peeled forward and fed imagery back to Dr. E in real time. A sudden swarm of aerial leech bots erupted from overhead vents and walls. The little things were ugly engineering. They had spider legs and claws designed to bite chassis and pierce suit nodes. They dove with one purpose: cling, suck, and destroy.

Zane reacted first. Chromatophore mode rippled across his suit, and he became a moving blur. A reflex net launched from his gauntlet, wrapped three bots, and dropped them to the ground. Tad ignited a plasma cutter like a sword and sliced a leech bot in half. The cavern was filled with smoke from molten alloy.

They pressed on and found the foyer: a wide, echoing room with glass tiles set into the floor and a row of observation windows looking into tanks. Rows of humanoid droids marched in patrolling patterns, swarmed by more leech bots. James' call came through measured and steady. "We have several hostiles."

The gauntlets glowed. Tidecore ignited their plasma swords on one side and TENDRILS launched from the other in ribbons of grappling motion. They coiled like living wire, snagging servo joints and yanking droids for teammates to disable. RaJohn vaulted between them, launching a net around a leech bot and sending it whirling. Sparks clawed the air. Plasma cutters for precise disabling, TENDRILS for restraint, and shock waves to stop motion, all combined into clean, surgical work. They left stacks of spent droids and scorched metal in their wake.

Past the foyer, lab corridors opened into rows of observation tanks. Juvenile sharks were housed in cylindrical tanks. Beyond them, lines of eels in tanks. Each network had a small, glowing parasitic cube attached to the base of the tank, encased in metal shielding. The sight was an indictment: Vex had weaponized life.

"Slow and clean ionic bursts first. Disrupt the node, then cut the mount," Dr. E said.

They worked like field medics. Tad moved with meticulous hands, plasma sword humming as he bored a gap in a welded ring and melted metal like lava. Zane slipped behind a rack, directed an ionic burst from one gauntlet, and severed a link at the base of a tank with his plasma cutter. Sparks flew. When a rig failed, the animal's vitals returned to normal, and the tank flushed it into the release channels back to open water.

At the far end of the floor, a production bay opened like a throat to the harbor. Massive assembly lines, racks of plated armor, crates of parasitic cubes, and a holo manifest scrolled a buyer list. Their stomachs tightened. This was a distribution. Copycat suits hung on racks, ready to be deployed. Shelves bore extra frames shaped like the silhouettes of Ironshade, Darkwake, Undertorque, Terrablight, Shatterborne, and Eclipse. Multiple examples meant additional threats. Down one corridor, several human hostages moaned with rigs attached to their heads and parasitic cubes above them. Above each one, a massive parasitic cube pulsed, centralizing power and mind control. This was control, power, deception, and complete submission. God came down to give life, but the enemy tries to suck everything pure out of it. The scale of Vex's plan hit hard. RaJohn, James, and Luna moved to set the hostages free. The light in their eyes had been dimming.

Then the lab lights shifted. A bank of observation windows flickered red as a central hub in a control room blinked awake. Vex stood on the other side of thick glass. The door beside the glass was a passkey card entry only. His voice filled the room through hard speakers, smooth and sick with curiosity. "You have excellent timing, Team TIDES," he said. "I was just about to finalize the protocol."

Puck deployed his plasma sword and began cutting into the thick glass to reach Dr. Vex. Suddenly, a countdown appeared on every HUD: ninety seconds. The hub's red grow-lights synchronized with blinking nodes. Upload windows. Network seeding. If the sequence completed, parasitic firmware would cascade outward, trying to override cube firmware and bury backdoors into networks wherever those cubes appeared.

"Break the relays," Hardee ordered. "No hostages left behind."

Jones and Zane spun into the relay corridors. The team covered the hostages and kept working to free them. "Wake up, you're safe now," Luna said as she slid a TIDE band onto a dazed wrist. The first relay went dark under Jones' TENDRIL microdisruptor. Sparks and static spat across the relay casing. Dr. E guided them like a surgeon, calling precise sequences to isolate and burn the parasitic handshake.

Then Eclipse arrived.

He moved like a smear of shadow, goo swirling and hissing from his gloves, the EMP symbol on his chest pulsing. "Well, it looks like you found a few new friends to dress up and play hero," he said. He leapt between gantries and released sizzle blasts that splattered walls and consoles. Black goo clung to a bulkhead reinforced wall, and it sizzled as his acid ate through.

Puck ordered, "Get those people out through the tunnel. Give all of them one of the extra Tide Bands to suit up in Frogman Mode."

Puck moved with a rapid set of Heart Core-driven motions, a TENDRIL throw to catch Eclipse's ankles, and a shot of sticky net to bind glove mechanics. Eclipse pressed his chest module a half click, and a small EMP burst stuttered across the room. Comms hiccupped, and the cavern filled with white noise. Eclipse sprayed a mist at a glob of goo on his right hand that ate it away at the goo and revealed machinery beneath. The Heart Core's pulse pushed through and rebounded the team's HRAM reflexes. Puck's TENDRIL stuck to a console beside Eclipse; he pulsed a microdisruptor down the line and sliced the last relay just before the upload window sealed. The red died. Eclipse roared, "Why do you always get in the way? Are you better than everyone else?"

Puck answered, "No, Christ in me is better."

Vex screamed a string of disgruntled syllables, and the base shook. He triggered bulkhead releases and manual failsafes.

Glass shuddered. Puck saw a glob of Eclipse's goo eating through a window, and water beginning to push through. He lobbed sticky nets and goo to slow the breach, then turned to find the exit. Eclipse and Vex were evacuating.

"You cannot stop the network," Vex snarled, but Puck heard fear under the words.

Eclipse scanned through the door, and they both sprinted to an underwater lock and boarded a fast, sealed submersible. Before the hatch slammed, Dr. Vex snarled, "You have undone the factory tonight. The network still grows."

Puck smashed through the mostly disabled glass and reached for the submersible, but there was no time to pursue. He fired a tethered micro-tracker as the craft screamed free; the tiny barnacle stuck to the hull. The sub vanished into the lock and out to open water. "Two are better than one," Puck chuckled.

Flood waters came like an animal. Rushing water punched through a breached wall eroded by Eclipse's black goo and poured into the lower corridor in a hungry sheet. Dr. E barked evac protocols. Tide bands flipped to ride-along. Rebreather visors locked down on hosts. Rose's cutter led the exit as Tidelink began receiving hostages in the tunnel throat exit into the harbor. Puck dove last and followed them out of the flooding base.

Puck watched the Kraken rise from the harbor and help Tidelink shepherd survivors toward the surface. A blast of water and air erupted from the corridor that had led down into the base. At the surface, by the docks, Brox and Ryan stabilized injuries with foam-based healing gel. Jonah cataloged manifests and evidence with a grim grin. At the same time, on higher ground, a handful of trench-coat cutouts were seized at the base entrance while ARC teams quarantined the rest of the day's catches.

Then Becker's HUD pinged. One last marker: a tiny metallic blip moving out of the harbor area on a county road. A truck. "We've got one crate on a truck. We keep an eye on the trackers, hopefully locating more of their operational sites." Becker said, voice low. "Let them lead us there."

Drones folded into pursuit. The Kraken's silhouette sank back into the water, an ocean promise kept. The team watched the blip fade away and then returned to work, checking pulses, securing evidence, and bundling the rescued into the chain that would carry them to Dr. Christenson. They had destroyed the factory, freed the animals, and captured enough to start finding answers, even though they had not caught all of the men who masterminded it. The truck blip and the sub meant the story had more pages.

Puck stood once, shoulder tight from the day that settled into night, and looked out to where the Kraken descended. He said softly, again not into the net but to the team who had everything folded into their chests, "Hold fast. We will finish this together. This isn't the end."

Back at the pier, the transports lifted, and the chain to ARC began. Jonah moved like it was second nature, logging every crate, every tag, stamping timestamps into the manifest. Hardee stepped forward to the waiting ARC reps and spoke the procedure out loud so there was no confusion.

"Two-signature transfer," he said. "I want itemized manifests TIDE-04A1 through TIDE-04A10. All evidence sealed. No asset moves without my clearance." Derrick uploaded copies to the Vaultrium hub.

Derrick tapped his console and confirmed. "Manifests uploaded. Copies to Dr. E and Celeste. Chain of custody initiated." Dr. E sent fast-moving octopods to transport. The octopods ripped through the tunnels at lightning speed. They could take the injured straight to Dr. Christenson thanks to the new tunnel entrance provided by old-school Team TIDES.

ARC officers checked tags, opened seals, and read out serials. One of them, austere and professional, scanned a crate and nodded. Hardee's gaze flicked from manifest to manifest. That is when an ARC tech reached into a bag and produced a small business card. The card bore a neat embossed sigil: a triangle pierced by a wave with a vertical line running down its center like a meridian.

Hardee glanced up. "Where did you get that?" he asked. The tech replied flatly, "Found it on one of the tall cutouts in a trench coat. He was at the warehouse out in front of the harbor for the meet when we nabbed him. Same sigil tattooed at the base of his neck. The Meridian Order. Self-righteous, purist. They call themselves the Prime Meridian. They think the world needs to be purged." He held the card out.

Hardee folded that detail into the log. "Note it. The Meridian Order. Tattoo on neck, business card. We'll flag shell companies linked to them. If any prisoners talk, get names and drop them to intel."

One of the prisoners, a wiry subject still strapped into a transport harness, muttered as he was lifted. Jonah leaned in. The man's voice was a rasp. "You took Stoggs' boys. That was a mistake." His eyes darted toward the road where one of the earlier trucks had pulled away. Hardee's jaw tightened. Jonah replied, "Yeah, well, Stoggs' boys were on a line to double-cross Stoggs. We saved him the trouble." The prisoner sneered, "That won't matter to Stoggs. He handles his own deals."

Meanwhile, in the Vaultrium, Celeste's voice broke on the comm. "Thank God," she said. "We saw every heartbeat on the feed. Families are safe for now. We have been praying for the teams." Dr. Zayler chimed in with clinical calm. "All vitals green on the dashboard." Shonté added, "We will keep the Tide Bands in Ride-Along Mode for the families. Those hostages were listed as missing. We have contacted their families so they can go to the hospital."

# The Quiet Gift of Dawn

Derrick reported on patients. "Vitals stable. Foam-based gel applied. We have people in medical pods inbound to the tunnel throat." Ryan added, "Ride-along is active on spare TIDE bands. Dr. E, transport pods in medical mode."

The octopods arrived, and the patients were loaded immediately. Tidecore was ready. Sun slid behind the low hills, and the harbor cooled under a silver moon as the team launched through the tunnels.

Puck, Tad, and Zane followed in Frogman Mode while the rest of Tidecore assisted inside the octopods with the patients. Looking back briefly, the Kraken lingered just outside the tunnel throat in the harbor, watching. Puck said, "Thanks, buddy. We really needed your help today," then focused on navigation and kicked into full HRAM Mode, boosting through the huge tunnels.

They arrived at the hospital bay soon after. TIDES hospital staff received the patients and immediately went to work. Dr. Christenson looked at the live feed and said, "Vitals on the medical transports look stable. Good job. We will give them a full exam in a little while. Why don't you go to the kitchen and grab something?"

Tidecore went into the kitchen where staff had food prepared and, of course, coffee. They powered down their suits, changed into plain clothes, and washed up. When they sat, it felt like a weight had been set down. "What a day," RaJohn said. "I never took off my biocast the other day since it fused with my nanos so seamlessly. I almost forgot it was even broken. I guess it is time to take it off." He chuckled and set the cast on the table. "No, no, not on the table," Luna teased. "Fancy nano cast biofluid doesn't go on tables. I will tell Shonté ." Laughter eased the soreness. They bowed their heads and thanked the Lord for safety, the mission, and the hostages. People held in bondage were set free today. That felt like victory.

After the meal and a few playful recaps, including Puck's Kraken ride, their TIDES' bands buzzed on their wrists.

A previous link was in range. They reengaged suits and moved outside toward the hospital harbor. The moon shone full and bright. Water rippled silver. A familiar shape rose in front of them, water streaming from its enormous head. The Kraken reached out a massive limb and brushed the team gently. Puck smiled. "What are we going to feed this guy?" he asked.

Dr. Christenson stepped out to check on the team and see how things were going. "Well, that's not something you see every day," he said.

"No, we kind of rescued him, and then he rescued everyone else. We were worried about feeding him," Puck said. Dr. Christenson laughed. "Don't you worry about that. We have resources. Agent Hardee and I have worked with people and animals for a long time. Let me make a quick call." He stepped away and dialed. A moment later, he turned back. "That's that," he said.

They explained the day's events and how Dr. Vex had twisted nature to his ends. "It's like Dr. Vex is the opposite of you, Dr. Christenson," Puck said.

Dr. Christenson nodded. "The enemy is an imitator, a copycat. What he does to creation is profane. Still, hope remains while a heart beats. Pray for your enemies to see the light."

Puck looked out over the harbor and up at the moon. He prayed quietly, "God bless our enemies. Give them the ability to see clearly, to see Your design in nature, and to come to the light. Let them repent and accept Your Son. In Jesus' name. Not our will, but your will, amen." The burdens of the day lifted and felt lighter. A helicopter approached and lowered a net trailing beneath it. The crew emptied a fresh haul of legal bycatch into a barge at the harbor. The Kraken fed like a patient king, then rolled and sent a slow plume of water into the moonlit air. It watched the shore and slipped back into the harbor like a promise kept for the night.

The team could hold fast until dawn, on the edge of morning. As the moon draws the tides together again and the harbor waits for the current to shift, the team had faith by night to last until first light. If God wills it, the great light will rise tomorrow. A new day would dawn. It is a quiet but powerful gift, and with it, the team would rise again to meet the battle on the horizon. For as long as the dawn rose over the waters, Team TIDES would rise with it, carrying the greater Light into the world.

Thank You for Joining the Adventure!
Your journey with Puck and his team doesn't have to end here!
By sharing your thoughts, you can inspire others to dive into this story and explore the limitless depths of their imagination.

📖 Write a Review

Your review makes a big difference! Share your favorite moments and why you enjoyed Frogman Puck Resurgent: The Turn of the Tides on Amazon, Goodreads, or your favorite review platform. Every word helps more readers discover this story!

🌐 Visit MJChanacapublishing.com

Explore our other books, download free guides, and sign up for updates on new releases and exclusive content.

📷 Connect and Share

Post your favorite scene, quote, or takeaway on social media with the hashtag #FrogmanPuck to join the conversation and inspire others.

I'm grateful for your support in bringing stories like Puck's to life. Together, we're building a community of faith-based life in action! You are not an accident, but have been designed for a purpose.

Stay connected and explore more exciting stories.
Follow Joel Chanaca on Amazon, Book Bub, and Goodreads!

Thank you for being part of this journey. The TIDES have turned- and so have our hearts! We can make a difference together. God bless you and the dreams He gives you.

**About the Author**

Joel Chanaca is a two-time Global Book Awards–winning author, recognized for his contributions to Humor and Heart and Hunter, the English Setter. A dedicated game warden with over twenty-five years of law enforcement experience, Joel has spent his career in public safety and wildlife law enforcement.

From an early age, Joel embraced adventure-camping, fishing, canoeing, and scuba diving-experiences that would later inspire his storytelling. His deep appreciation for nature has only grown through his work in natural resource protection, reinforcing his belief in the beauty and complexity of God's creation.

"The elements of design are all around us. If we take the time to pause and look, we can see how God has made a place for us. More than just the wonders of the earth, His plan extends beyond the physical world. Through Christ, we are offered the ultimate gift of salvation-a sacrifice made so that He could prepare a place for us beyond what we can see."

**Your Honest Review Makes a Difference**

"I hope Frogman Puck Resurgent: Turn of the Tides has captured part of the adventure in your spirit towards your walk with God. Keep up the good fight by keeping close to the Word of God, your greatest weapon."

Thank you,

Joel

# Frogman Puck

# Origins

Join our launch team at
MJChanacapublishing.com and receive our
content for free while space is still
available.

# Frogman Puck

## Reckoning

## The Edge of Dawn

Night of the Meridian: Horizon of Justice

**Joel Chanaca**

www.ingramcontent.com/pod-product-compliance
Lightning Source LLC
Chambersburg PA
CBHW051143120626
46547CB00012B/921